BIG PHARMA, BIG GREED
The inside story of one lawyer's battle to stem the flood of dangerous medicines and protect public health

Stephen A. Sheller, Esq.
with Sidney D. Kirkpatrick
and Chris Mondics

WASHINGTON D.C.

Visit www.ANationBetrayed.com for updates, news, video, and more.

"The main reason we take so many drugs is that drug companies don't sell drugs; they sell lies about drugs."

—Dr. Peter Gøtzsche, professor of clinical research design and analysis and director of the Nordic Cochrane Center

Copyright © 2018 Stephen A. Sheller, Sidney D. Kirkpatrick, and Chris Mondics

All rights reserved.

No part of this book may be reproduced, in any form, without written permission from the author.

Requests for permission to reproduce selections from this book should be mailed to: Strong Arm Press, 1440 G St NW, Washington, D.C. 20005

Published in the United States by Strong Arm Press, 2018

www.strongarmpress.com

ISBN-13: 978-1-947492-27-1

Contents

Introduction: Death by Prescription 1
Chapter 1: How the Fox Got in the Henhouse 10
Chapter 2: Your Prozac Is in the Mail 17
Chapter 3: The "Cure" May Be The Problem 32
Chapter 4: Whistleblowers Speak Up 39
Chapter 5: Indicting Big Pharma 44
Chapter 6: When One Antidepressant Isn't Enough 48
Chapter 7: Exposing the Betrayal 53
Chapter 8: The Boy Who Grew Breasts 58
Chapter 9: Following the Money 63
Chapter 10: Risperdal and the Downstream Effects 67
Chapter 11: Band-Aids, Baby Shampoo, and Big Pharma 78
Chapter 12: Pharma's P's: Politicians, Physicians, and Pharmacists 81
Chapter 13: The FDA: Federal Drug Accomplice 85
Chapter 14: Culpability in the Courts 94
Chapter 15: Holding Pharma Execs to Account 105
Afterword: Taking back control from Big Pharma 115
Acknowledgments 128
About The Authors 130
Notes 141

INTRODUCTION: DEATH BY PRESCRIPTION

On April 16, 2009, seven-year-old Gabriel Myers locked himself in the bathroom of his suburban Florida foster home, coiled a detachable shower hose around his neck, and hung himself. A bright and charming little boy with close-cropped blond hair and brown eyes, Gabriel was acting out, his behavior having spiraled out of control over the previous year. The police investigation would reveal a tragedy nearly beyond belief: child service caseworkers were medicating him with adult doses of antipsychotic drugs, the negative side effects of which include an increased risk of suicide and violent behavior.

Prescription drug therapy for young Gabriel hadn't begun in Florida but back in Ohio, where he was living with his grandparents while his mother, Candace, was serving jail time. Gabriel, four years old at the time, had begun wetting his bed and acting out in the classroom. On the recommendation of a school therapist, he was diagnosed with attention deficit hyperactivity disorder, or ADHD, and put on Adderall XR, an amphetamine that is popularly prescribed to children and teens to enhance concentration in the classroom. The drug may have temporarily masked the symptoms Gabriel was being treated for, but the root cause of his misbehavior wasn't something chemical stimulants could remedy. It rarely is. Gabriel had repeatedly been molested at knifepoint by a 12-year-old schoolmate. An abuse report was filed two years after the sexual abuse occurred with no follow-up. By the time state authorities were made aware of Gabriel's molestation, he was living with his mother in Florida.[1]

Gabriel came to the attention of police in 2008, when Broward County patrolmen found his mother, Candace, unconscious in her car parked behind a Denny's restaurant. In the front seat beside her, they found powder and crack cocaine along with Xanax and Oxycodone in unmarked pharmaceutical containers. Gabriel, then age six, was in the backseat. The Florida Department of Children and Families took custody of Gabriel pending legal proceedings against his mother. Gabriel's father, Rocky Newman, was serving time in a Florida prison and therefore unable to care for him. For the next 11 months, Gabriel would be a ward of the state.[2]

During his initial evaluation with child services, Gabriel was forth- coming about his mother's drug addiction and the molestation he had suffered in Ohio. He was again diagnosed with ADHD and was this time placed on the next-generation amphetamine, Vyvanse. Though it was only approved for use by adults, Vyvanse could, like the vast majority of drugs used to treat ADD and ADHD, be prescribed to a child "off-label" with a physician's approval. This allows doctors to prescribe the drug if they think it's the best option for a patient even though the FDA has not approved the medication for a specific condition or a certain class of people, in this case children.

However, rather than enhancing Gabriel's ability to behave in the classroom, the drug cocktail made him more agitated and disruptive.

Gabriel's foster parents and schoolteachers reported more extreme behavioral outbursts; he was inappropriately touching other students and squirted classmates with red dye from a spray bottle. Gabriel was prescribed a combination of Lexapro, used to treat anxiety disorders in teens and adults, and Zyprexa, an antipsychotic that was approved by the FDA for adults with schizophrenia. Both of these drugs are known to increase the risk of violence and suicide. Patients sometimes suffer sudden mood swings and an inability to control rage. Gabriel's court-appointed psychiatrist apparently didn't know or take the trouble to investigate.

In the last few days of his life, the seven-year-old told classmates that he felt a strong desire to kill people but didn't have a plan in mind. His teachers reported that he sometimes appeared dazed in class and would trip, fall, or walk into things. At other times, he would suddenly laugh or cry uncontrollably. His medication was changed once more, this time to Symbyax, a powerful Zyprexa compound mixed with Prozac. He was also informed by child services caseworkers that his mother would no longer have visitation rights and that he would be relocated to Ohio, where the alleged molestation had occurred.

On the day before he took his own life, Gabriel complained of severe stomach problems, was lightheaded and nauseous, and vomited in the school lunchroom. He was excused from classes and didn't return to school the next day. Though state law mandated that he be supervised by a foster parent or certified caregiver, he was home alone with his foster father's 19-year-old son, who was not trained or equipped to handle an emergency situation. At lunchtime, Gabriel tossed the meal that had been prepared for him into the kitchen trash can, announced that he was going to take his own life, and locked himself in the bathroom.

Responsibility for Gabriel's suicide can reasonably be shared by many, foremost among them his own parents, who were clearly unable to care for their son. However, there were many opportunities for intervention by those who were charged with protecting him. Had police investigated Gabriel's sexual-abuse claims in a timelier way, he might have been put under the supervision of a therapist who was specifically trained to address his particular needs. A subsequent investigation substantiated Gabriel's story, but not in time to do the most good or save other children from a teenage sexual predator at large in an Ohio elementary school. Florida authorities also didn't request a copy of his child welfare history in Ohio, which would have presumably helped caseworkers and teachers better understand why the child felt compelled to act out.

Most troubling of all was how Gabriel had been medicated for the last year of his life. Rather than deal with the root cause of his behavior, his court-appointed psychiatrist medicated him with powerful psychotropic drugs used to sedate adult patients. As the police investigation revealed, the psychiatrist spent no more than a few minutes with the boy before prescribing him these medications and, when later questioned by reporters, said that he could not specifically recall Gabriel as he was one of many foster children in his care. Lack of a proper interview, however, did not prevent the psychiatrist from writing prescriptions that increased the likelihood of violent behavior. Moreover, permission to administer these drugs was not obtained from Gabriel's mother or the courts, as mandated by state law. The only document on record was a generic medical release signed by Candace on the night police found her unconscious from a drug overdose.[3]

Although it is abundantly clear that Gabriel fell between the cracks and didn't get the help he clearly needed, the sad truth is that his story is not uncommon. Twenty million children in the United States today are diagnosed with mental disorders for which psychiatrists prescribe antipsychotic drugs. The checklist of behaviors these children suffer from—highlighted on drug-company-sponsored parent questionnaires found on the Internet or in literature in pediatric waiting rooms—are often minor and sometimes include child appropriate actions such as "losing too many pencils," "does not listen to his teachers," "can't sit still in his chair," and "runs about or climbs excessively." What was once considered normal child and adolescent behavior has now been elevated to conditions for which drugs are recommended in one-third of all pediatric psychiatrist evaluations. These drugs expose children to side effects that can be far worse than the condition for which they are prescribed. Among these side effects are Parkinson's-like symptoms, extreme weight gain, diabetes, female-like breast growth in men and boys, psychosis, suicide, and a condition that's sometimes referred to as an "urge to kill."

Let's not forget the murder of 12 students and a teacher and the wounding of 26 others at Columbine High School. At least one, and possibly both, of the two shooters was being medicated with psychiatric drugs.[4] More recently, there was the case of Aaron Alexis, whose murderous rampage at the Washington Navy Yard in September 2013 left 12 dead. The psychiatric medication he was being given came with an equally dire list of potential side effects, which include mania, paranoia, psychosis, hallucinations, and self-destructive behavior.

Less than three years before Gabriel Myers took his own life, four- year-old Rebecca Riley, diagnosed with ADHD, died in her Massachusetts home of a drug overdose of the antipsychotics Seroquel and Depakote. Rebecca's teachers reported that she appeared to be so medicated that she had to be helped walking up the stairs and sitting in her chair at preschool.[5] Seven months before Riley's death, three-year-old Destiny Hager from Council Grove, Kansas, died from taking

Seroquel, Geodon, and Risperdal among other powerful adult antipsychotics prescribed to children with attention deficit disorders. Her psychiatrist had also placed six other youngsters on antipsychotics, including one two-year-old, two three-year-olds, and a four-year-old.[6] And these are merely the cases that make the headlines. The vast majority of children's deaths from psychiatric drugs go unreported. I hear about them because the families of victims visit my law office and tellme their stories, wanting my help and counsel.

The tragedy is that I know the deaths of these children could have been prevented. Five years before Gabriel's suicide, I filed multiple lawsuits aimed at keeping these drugs from being prescribed to children. My litigation resulted in our firm winning the largest settlement ever paid by one defendant, Eli Lilly, for its marketing of Zyprexa. In presenting our case, I submitted overwhelming documentary evidence and sworn testimony describing how Lilly had knowingly manipulated test results that were presented to the U.S. Food and Drug Administration (FDA) and had assembled dedicated sales teams to illegally sell Zyprexa to children. Within a 15-month period, I had also successfully won settlements against AstraZeneca for its illicit sales of Seroquel and against Pfizer for its marketing of Geodon and other drugs. I would subsequently win another record-breaking settlement from Johnson & Johnson over its marketing campaigns for Risperdal and Invega.

These pharmaceutical giants have spent billions of dollars illegally targeting their sales campaigns at patients their drugs were not approved for and for whom there was no medical evidence that they were effective. Kickbacks and other incentives have been paid to physicians, most notably to child psychiatrists, caring for foster children. Pharmaceutical company marketing departments, not independent and impartial researchers, write reviews of these drugs for the major medical journals. And making matters worse, our regulatory agencies contribute to the deceit. As former FDA scientist Leo Lutwak said, "If the American people knew some of the things thatwent on at the FDA, they'd never take anything but Bayer aspirin."[7]

The evidence of pharmaceutical industry deception is overwhelming, and it seems, grows by the day.

On Aug. 8, 2018, in a hearing before Philadelphia Common Pleas Court Judge Arthur New, our legal team presented evidence that Janssen Pharmaceuticals had engaged in a decades-long deception aimed at hiding the dangers of Risperdal from unsuspecting parents whose children had been given the drug off label for a variety of supposed behavior disorders.

Going back as far as 2003, Janssen had clinical trial data showing the risk of young boys given Risperdal for developing gynecomastia, a condition in which they develop permanent female breast tissue, was as high as 12.5 percent.

Yet on the medication's 2006 FDA approved warning label, the overall risk of adverse events was placed at 2.3 percent while the incidence of gynecomastia was described as rare. In 2003, in furtherance of this deception, company marketing staff prepared a research paper for the Journal of American Psychiatry purporting to show that there was no linkage at all between the drug and the development of female breast tissue in boys.

The company manipulated data to downplay the risk by, in one calculation, reducing the numerator of adolescent boys with gynecomastia while including in the study a group of older boys and females, a group with a lower risk. The manipulation resulted in a gynecomastia rate of less than one percent when the actual incidence was 4.4 percent. The company then drafted a scientific article, published in the Journal of Clinical Psychiatry, that lent credence to the idea that there was no linkage between the drug and gynecomastia, even though it had internal study results showing otherwise.

"I grew up in the Frankford section of the city and in Frankford we called that a lie," said Philadelphia lawyer, Charles Becker, during arguments in August 2018 in a lawsuit alleging Janssen had concealed the risks. "We call that something you would get into trouble with your mother about."

Although much of the work on the article was done by Janssen, two prominent scientists, Denis Daneman, a Toronto based pediatrician and Robert Findling, a U.S. based child psychiatrist, agreed to be named as co-authors.[8]

Some thirteen years later, following an onslaught of lawsuits, the company reanalyzed the data used for the Journal of American Psychiatry article claiming that it had confirmed the original findings of no risk. Daneman and Findling, meanwhile, issued a statement saying the 2003 article had been largely verified.[9]

The sad truth is that my litigation didn't save the life of Gabriel Myers. Eli Lilly paid an enormous amount of money to settle the case, and for a few months, the company's stock traded lower on the New York Stock Exchange. Investors, not corporate executives, paid the price. Also, for a time, the negative side effects of Zyprexa and its marketing to children made front page news. The same was true of our settlements with AstraZeneca, Pfizer, and Johnson & Johnson. Yet despite the landmark multibillion-dollar settlements to compensate for the harm done to patients and taxpayers, no corporate decision makers went to jail. These companies didn't have to publicly reveal what they had done and neither were the vast majority of documents we submitted to the courts ever made public, a consequence of protective orders imposed by courts all too sympathetic to the wishes of Big Pharma.

Today, all of these drugs—Zyprexa, Seroquel, Geodon, Risperdal, and Invega along with newer and more dangerous antipsychotics such as Abilify—are still on the market and are routinely prescribed to children who are, in my opinion, too young to legitimately be diagnosed as suffering from the psychotic disorders for which these drugs have been approved. Test results of a medicine's side effects are routinely deemed to be proprietary information and hence not available to consumers, prosecutors, or even the FDA, the institution charged with regulating these drugs.

Congress failed to ratify legislation that would have called for increased drug monitoring and closer supervision of children in foster care and other publicly funded programs on the grounds that doing so would place undue burden on the pharmaceutical industry—never mind seven-year-old Gabriel Myers, four-year-old Rebecca Riley, nor toddler Destiny Hager.

In the legal climate we live in, a corporation's right to free speech, even when it's proven to be lies, often trumps the rights of consumers. Just ask our current United States Supreme Court.

The courts and our government regulators delivered a clear message: even though the pharmaceutical companies illegally marketed their antipsychotics and knowingly withheld drug studies that might have reasonably resulted in their removal from pharmacy shelves, the government declared that these companies could, after all, go ahead and sell them to children. Apparently, the taxpayer-funded psychiatrist who had prescribed them to Gabriel Myers also wasn't at fault, which is why today he not only still has his medical license, but also has a thriving practice treating foster children.[10]

If this sounds unfair, it's because it is. If this doesn't make common sense, it's because it doesn't. It's the reality where we, as a nation, have found ourselves. Betrayals of the public trust have become so commonplace that the vast majority of us have begun taking injustice for granted. We accept lies even when we know we are being lied to. We accept the empty promises of reform with deep-seated cynicism and believe we are powerless to do anything about it.

I do think we have choices, though.

Rather than throwing up our hands in resignation or taking to the streets in angry and unfocused protest, it's possible to direct our outrage in ways that can and do make a difference. I know because I've succeeded in doing this in the courtroom—not to the extent or as effectively as I would have liked but long enough to know that justice can and will ultimately triumph when the truth is exposed. As I have sought to convey in these pages, fighting for justice demands a willingness to carefully examine the facts, think clearly about the nature of the betrayal, understand what can be done about it, and find a solution that will do the most good. Democracy is not a spectator sport. The powerful corporate and government forces that minimize the less powerful must be challenged, even in the face of overwhelming odds. This is why I'm writing this book and why I'm back in court fighting on behalf of Gabriel Myers and thousands of children like him.

I'll not rest until I've exposed the truth. Nor should you.

STEPHEN A. SHELLER

CHAPTER 1: HOW THE FOX GOT IN THE HENHOUSE

Bringing about justice must not be perceived as a matter of winning or losing, but by whether or not a wrong has been righted. By focusing on in justice and what can be done about it, the rest takes care of itself. The reason I have been successful, I believe, is by not losing sight of why I became a lawyer: a burning desire to fight for what's right and just.

My life has been made up of threads: clients, judges, judicial decisions (some good and some bad)—all have shaped the lawyer I've become. I began as a young idealist helping to fight for civil rights in the 1960s, and later as a litigator I was unafraid to take on what some others considered impossible challenges, like voter fraud litigation in the 2000 presidential elections.

Spanning more than five decades, the threads of my career canvas have woven a path to the point at which I now stand, hoping to shed light on the ills of a pharmaceutical industry run amok. But before that story, I must tell you this one. One that begins in 2000 with a phone call and closes out that decade with the third-largest drug settlement in U.S history.

Like so many of my cases that start out as issues affecting my friends, my family and our coworkers and gradually spread into the larger community, my voter fraud investigation was triggered by a telephone call, in this case from my mother-in-law, Bobbie Mitnik, in Palm Beach County, Florida. She phoned my office in Philadelphia on Election Day, Nov. 7, 2000, to express her deep concern that the ballot on the punch vote recorder at her polling station was so confusing she couldn't be certain if she had voted for Democrat Al Gore or ultraconservative Reform Party Candidate Pat Buchanan. Not only that, she said the pre-election instruction booklet she received in the mail, which contained a sample ballot she had filled out at home, was laid out differently than the one displayed on the Votomatic vote recorder in the polling booth.

Upset, Bobbie asked me what could be done. I followed up our conversation with phone calls to friends and other family in Palm Beach and discovered that Bobbie's experience wasn't unique. Other elderly Floridians in that county had encountered the same problem.

The infamous "butterfly ballot," as it was later known, hadn't listed the three presidential candidates' names one atop the other on a single page as had been done elsewhere in Florida but, instead, had put Gore's and Buchanan's names on different pages opposite one another, making it difficult for the voter to know where they should punch the card for the candidate of their choice.

I can be accused of many things, but sitting on my hands is not one of them. First on my agenda was calling my friend Ed Rendell, the former Philadelphia mayor, future governor of Pennsylvania, and at that time the chair of the Democratic National Committee. Rendell agreed I should "get down there, figure it out, and see what could be done." On my own dime, of course.

Forty-eight hours later, Florida friends and colleagues Dave Krathen and Gary Farmer joined me at the Palm Beach County Courthouse to file a class action suit seeking to enjoin the certification of the Palm Beach County vote by Katherine Harris, the Republican Secretary of State. We couldn't have imagined that what began with my mother-in-law's telephone call would mushroom into multiple state and federal complaints that would ultimately result in a post-election battle in the U.S. Supreme Court.

In addition to the controversial ballot layout, which had possibly been designed to mislead voters into casting their ballots for candidates not of their choosing, serious other questions were being raised. Many thousands of votes hadn't been counted because the pointer or stylus used in the Votomatic punch card machine hadn't cleanly penetrated the ballot. If a hole in the ballot card was not cleanly punched through, leaving the much-discussed "hanging" or "dimpled chads," the tabulating machines didn't count the vote.

Miscast votes, however, were not the only problem. As the Miami Herald would later confirm, voters in Palm Beach County were 100 times more likely than elsewhere in South Florida to invalidate their votes by voting for both Gore and Buchanan.[11]

Allegations of fraud and misconduct continued unabated. I didn't yet know the full extent of the behind-the-scenes decisions that contributed to the faulty Palm Beach vote, but I suspected that we were onto something.

More than anything else, we had to educate the public about what had taken place. The challenges of doing so in such a short time frame were daunting, and our opposition had all the advantages. George W. Bush, brother of the governor of Florida, Jeb Bush, had technically already won the election, and Katherine Harris, the Secretary of State of the Commonwealth of Florida, was co-chair of Bush's Florida election committee.

By November 14, the day of our first court appearance, the press was reporting allegations of electoral fraud throughout the state. Improper ballot design and defective equipment combined to create a flawed election, and a flawed election was what Palm Beach got. The county became ground zero in the post-election controversy. Thousands of protesters, mostly African Americans, angry because so many of their votes hadn't been counted, had descended upon Palm Beach. The largest contingent of protesters, led by Reverend Jesse Jackson, marched in the streets and camped out in front of the courthouse, calling, as we did, for the vote recount to be resumed and for a full-fledged nonpartisan inquiry into the butterfly ballots.

I felt a mix of emotions: a tremendous desire to remain steadfast in my commitment to represent my mother-in-law and so many more thousands of disenfranchised Florida voters, and trepidation that a pitched battle between protestors and police would overshadow what we sought to accomplish in court.

Years earlier, amid demonstrations outside the Philadelphia courthouse, I had defended the Black Panthers on trumped-up murder and conspiracy charges. I had joined protest marches and demonstrations with the Congress of Racial Equality (CORE) while leading the court battle for higher wages, healthy working conditions, and gender equality on behalf of black janitorial trade unions and maids. Thanks to suits that I brought on behalf of the American Civil Liberties Union (ACLU), we won the rights for young people to vote in the ward where they lived while going to college if it differed from their home residences, and drafted inclusive new rules that were used to determine the selection of delegates for presidential conventions.

I don't mention these things to beat my own drum or display my left-leaning liberal roots, but to put our greater national struggle into historical perspective. The sense of anger and betrayal that I felt in Palm Beach was made the more acute because I, a Jew from Brooklyn, and so many others of my generation—whites and blacks and Jews and Gentiles—had fought this battle before. Civil and voter rights legislation was our generation's legacy. There I was, nearly 40 years later, fighting to reclaim lost ground. I was dumbfounded by what came next as one judge after another recused themselves from hearing our case. The recusals continued into the next day until, to our relief, Judge Jorge Labarga took the assignment.

Frustratingly, 27 days later, our case wasn't the one that reached the U.S. Supreme Court. While our Palm Beach litigation came first and was, I believe, the strongest case, the battle over the presidential election had spread into other, much larger counties throughout the state. Eventually, Al Gore's team asked us to withdraw our complaint on behalf of the citizens of Palm Beach County in favor of a new one filed by David Boies on behalf of Al Gore who by then joined the fray.

My decision to stand down turned out to be the most regrettable of my entire career, for the stakes couldn't have been higher. Knowing in hindsight what we do about the Bush presidency, I should not have left it in the hands of others to fight to uphold our nation's civil rights—protections which I would soon see cast aside in favor of thinly veiled and self-serving corporate interests.

I don't wish to burden you with every fine detail of how I believe voter fraud was engineered in Florida, but as you will see in the chapters to come, the key to understanding the truth of a betrayal is often less a matter of legal reasoning than it is unraveling the tangled knot of the facts of a case.

As a result of the "stolen" 2000 election, I believe our nation was led into two needless wars instead of one warranted police action. Had Bush not taken office, we may not have been saddled with draconian Voter ID and redistricting laws that have disenfranchised hundreds of thousands of voters. Under a different chief executive, we might not have a judiciary that increasingly operates on a two-tier system of justice—one for the well off and one for the poor.

With a different chief executive, we may not have had a Supreme Court that decided in favor of Citizen's United, in which corporations have been granted corporate personhood with constitutional rights similar to yours and mine, including that of free speech.

I'll not argue that some or all of these things wouldn't have occurred had Gore, not Bush, sat in the Oval Office, or that Democrats aren't also responsible for many of our nation's travails. But I can tell you with absolute certainty that the 2000 election brought forth a massive tidal wave of corporate influence that infected our government at all levels. Nowhere is this more evident than with the pharmaceutical industry chieftains, whose lobbyists became key players in the Bush administration, and under whose influence the U.S. Food and Drug Administration became the "fast drug approval" agency.

Among the most powerful of those pharmaceutical corporations is Eli Lilly and Co., which Gary Farmer and I would take to court in the same state where we had earlier filed voter fraud charges. That case became the genesis of the litigation described in these pages. In retrospect, our choice to team up and take on Lilly was providential—either that or a recipe for disaster. Not only were members of the Bush family major stockholders in Eli Lilly and other pharmaceutical companies, they were beholden to the industry in other ways as well.

After leaving his post as head of the Central Intelligence Agency in 1977, George H. W. Bush was appointed a director on Lilly's board, an honor bestowed upon him by the wealthy and influential father of future Vice President Dan Quayle, the owner of a controlling interest in the company.

Then, and later, Bush senior would successfully lobby to permit drug companies to sell obsolete or domestically banned pharmaceuticals to Third World countries. Between 1981 and 1989, while serving as vice president under Ronald Reagan, Bush would continue to act on behalf of pharmaceutical company interests by personally requesting the IRS to give special tax breaks for Lilly and other drug companies.[12]

Also serving on Lilly's board of directors was Bush 2000 campaign contributor Ken Lay, the former CEO of Enron who President George W. Bush and the First Lady joined on a corporate jet on their first trip to Washington after winning the election. All of us know, of course, what happened there: Enron would go on to become the posterchild of institutionalized, systematic and creatively planned accounting fraud, which would set the stage for the Wall Street subprime mortgage crisis of 2008.

As would soon become evident to Gary and me, the Bush connection to Eli Lilly and the Big Pharma "alumni club" ran much deeper than this. Mitch Daniels, a former vice president of Lilly, became Bush's director of management and budget. Sidney Taurel, another former Lilly CEO, would join Bush's Homeland Security Advisory Council. Secretary of Defense Donald Rumsfeld served on the board of Lilly partners Amylin Pharmaceuticals and Gilead Sciences Inc.

Over the years of the Bush presidency, there was a revolving door between administration veterans and Lilly's senior management. Among them was Alex Azar, Bush's deputy secretary of the Department of Health and Human Services who oversaw such agencies as the FDA, the National Institutes of Health (NIH), the Centers for Disease Control (CDC), and the Centers for Medicare & Medicaid Services (CMS). Azar would become the senior vice president of corporate affairs and communication for Lilly after leaving his government post and later president of Lilly USA, the company's biggest unit.

Then there was Big Pharma's relentless defender, Dr. Andrew von Eschenbach, whom the younger President Bush appointed as head of the National Cancer Institute and who he would later tap to head the FDA. As the Union of Concerned Scientists and the National Academies of Sciences, Engineering, and Medicine's Institute of

Medicine would report in 2006, under Eschenbach's tenure the agency was "perverting science for political and financial bene- factors."[13]

Care to guess which drug company dominated the lobbying pack? In our new pharmaceutical litigation, Gary and I encountered so many conflicts of interest that our case could have been justifiably called Lillygate.

CHAPTER 2: YOUR PROZAC IS IN THE MAIL

Had I not received that providential telephone call from my mother- in-law in Palm Beach, and subsequently teamed-up with Gary Farmer to file *Bush v. Gore*, I might never have known about a highly unorthodox 2002 Florida scheme to market a new Eli Lilly drug, Prozac Weekly—which triggered a tsunami of pharmaceutical litigation to come. Rather than just advertising Prozac Weekly in the usual ways and trying to impress upon prescribers the drug's alleged new benefits, Lilly caused free samples to be sent directly to potential customers.

The inciting event that first caught our attention was a package sent in April 2002 from a Walgreens Pharmacy in Deerfield, Florida, to a 58-year-old caregiver who lived nearby. I'll call her "S.K." to protect what little privacy she has left. Included in the package were four bright, multi-colored capsules, which, as S.K. later said, looked like candy and could have been ingested by her grandchildren had they opened the unsolicited mailing.

In addition to the capsules, enclosed was a letter from Holy Cross Medical Group, a subsidiary of Holy Cross Hospital in Fort Lauderdale. The missive was signed by Lise Lambert, S.K.'s doctor, and three colleagues from the same medical group. It read:

Dear Patient, we are very excited to be able to offer you a more convenient way to take your antidepressant medication. Prozac Weekly is the exact same medication as Prozac, but with convenient, once-a-week dosing.

For your convenience, enclosed you will find a FREE one-month trial of Prozac Weekly. If you wish to try Prozac Weekly, stop your daily antidepressant one day before starting Prozac Weekly; then take only Prozac Weekly once a week thereafter.

Congratulations on being one step closer to full recovery.

If you have any questions or concerns, please call our office at your earliest convenience.

S.K. was mystified and disturbed. She had undergone treatment for depression for a number of years, a condition that she didn't want publicized lest it make employers wary of hiring her. About eight years earlier, she had been given a prescription for Prozac, which she had filled at a Walgreens. However, that was in Massachusetts, and since her move to Florida, she'd had no dealings with Walgreens. That she was sent Prozac at all was beyond her comprehension. In the past, she had a bad reaction to it, forcing her psychiatrist to prescribe an alternative antidepressant. Not only that, she hadn't seen Dr. Lambert for months, nor had any discussions with her about changing her medication. Why would her former physician have Walgreens send her a drug to which she would likely have an allergic reaction?

Had she not had an unfortunate experience with Prozac, she said she might well have taken the free pills, though the mailing contained no warnings about the many adverse effects or descriptions of medical conditions that made use of Prozac inadvisable. For example, pregnant women taking Prozac and several other selective serotonin reuptake inhibitors (SSRIs) run the serious risk of delivering babies with heart defects, and for everyone taking the drugs there's an increased risk of suicide. The final sentence inviting "Dear Patient" to call the office with questions or concerns could hardly constitute a product warning, especially when immediately preceded by the congratulatory "step to full recovery" line.

The more S.K. considered her gift, the more alarmed she became. She had no doubt that others had also received it. The "Dear Patient" salutation indicated that it had not come from her personal physician, nor could she imagine her doctor, nor other doctors for that matter, using the word "free" in capital letters, much less the term "congratulations." The whole thing smelled of an advertising promotion for a prescription drug, which meant it was likely mailed to a wide swath of people, some of whom would, like her, react poorly to Prozac but would take the free capsules because they would assume their doctors would never send them anything harmful. She decided to see Gary Farmer in Fort Lauderdale. Farmer's expertise was not product liability nor class-action law, but he knew it was mine. Pharmaceutical company fraud and misbehavior was one of my specialties.

"You aren't going to believe this" was how he began our conversation. Gary was right. It was stranger than fiction. Here was a drug company bypassing physicians and its own sales reps by taking its mind-altering antidepressants directly to the consumer.

I hadn't yet thought through what laws were being broken, but it was surely beyond the scope of ethical behavior. Not only had S.K.'s personal medical records been somehow made public, but that information was also being used to market prescription medication directly to her by mail no less. This had nothing to do with "treating her condition," as the letter suggested. It had everything to do with generating profits.

Soon thereafter, we received a call from a woman whose sixteen-year-old son received extended release Prozac in the mail. He had never been prescribed the drug. Were we looking at a tsunami of prescription drugs being sent unsolicited by one of the largest drug manufacturers in the country?

As Gary and I soon learned, there was already litigation over Prozac, and nearly all of it centered on the drug's negative side effects. Most notable was a case in Kentucky that didn't get much media attention but spoke volumes about the minefield we were about to walk into.

The case involved a 47-year-old printer who, one month after he began taking Prozac, opened fire at his workplace with an AK-47. The surviving victims of the slaughter sued Lilly, claiming that an adverse reaction to Prozac had pushed the shooter over the edge. Among the revelations to emerge during the trial were previously undisclosed clinical tests linking Prozac to sudden and extreme episodes of violence in some users.[14] These tests had apparently not been submitted to the FDA during the drug approval process. Or had they? As it was also revealed at this trial, five of the nine FDA scientists charged with investigating Prozac were on Big Pharma's payroll, and two had actually conducted Prozac clinical trials for Lilly. And even these revelations couldn't compare to what the presiding judge would discover after the case was settled in Lilly's favor.

Similar to the surprise ending in a John Grisham novel, the judge discovered that Lilly had cut a secret deal with the plaintiff's attorneys not to introduce corporate business records, drug trial results, and company correspondence into the public record.[15] Lilly would ultimately have to pay a penalty for collusion with opposing counsel, but unfortunately for those who took Lilly's drugs, the company was not forced to make public the documents it had gone to such lengths to hide.

Perhaps Gary and I could somehow make public whatever Lilly had to hide in our new case. As I've said and will repeat again, big things can come out of small first steps.

Based on what I've written so far, you might say that I don't think very highly of pharmaceutical industry practices and that I have serious reservations about the FDA's ability to regulate it. You would be right. This doesn't mean, however, that I don't understand the miracle of modern science or appreciate the contributions that the industry has brought to the world. HIV has gone from a death sentence to a chronic disease. Heart bypasses and the drugs that make them possible have saved the lives of many of my friends. My problem begins when marketers, not scientists, become the decision makers, and dollars and cents trump health concerns. And this case, with its direct-to-the-consumer marketing of drugs, seemed to be the epitome of all that was wrong with the industry.

Based on what we were learning, Gary and I filed a class action lawsuit in Florida state court with S.K. and others as plaintiffs. The defendants were Walgreens, the hospital, its group practice, and its practitioners, along with Indianapolis-based Eli Lilly. Our lawsuit made news not only in Fort Lauderdale but was also picked up by the Associated Press and the *Wall Street Journal*. It also hit the front page of the *New York Times*, where I was quoted as saying, "What they should be doing is developing a drug to diminish their greed."[16]

I used the same or similar response when the media came calling. S.K. and I were interviewed on ABC's *Good Morning America*, on CBS's *Early Show*, on CNN, and on NPR. It struck me that the media's strong reaction was largely based on shock: until then, it had just never occurred to most people that a drugstore would mail free samples of a prescription drug, let alone one as powerful and, I believe, addictive as Prozac. Doctors often give out samples, but when they do, they are there to discuss the medication with the patient, and the drug itself is accompanied by the required warnings.

Following an onslaught of bad publicity created by the suit, the defendants dove for cover. Holy Cross Hospital, its medical group, and the medical group's staff took refuge in silence. Walgreens claimed it had been given prescriptions for the samples and certainly never would have mailed them if it hadn't. Moreover, the company said, it received coupons from Eli Lilly to be submitted for reimbursement. If anyone was to blame, it was Eli Lilly, or so the rationale went.

Lilly, in turn, faulted four overzealous pharmaceutical reps for coming up with the entire marketing scheme and presumably for paying for the printing and the free Prozac mailing out of their own pockets. They were subsequently fired and later sued Lilly for wrongful termination, claiming they were just following orders. Even if it had been their idea, it's difficult to understand why Lilly would be upset with them, as it's been maintaining since our suit was filed that the mailings signed by physicians were "well intentioned and perfectly appropriate conduct."

For at least seven months prior to the day S.K. got her free gift, other patients had also received free prescriptions for Prozac Weekly. Among them was 16-year-old M.G., who came home from school to discover his free package of Prozac Weekly, sent with a letter from the head doctor of the family practice that he and his mother went to in West Palm Beach. M. G. was confused. He was not taking an antidepressant and never had. He said he had "no clue" where the sender would get the idea that he wanted or needed Prozac Extended Release. Then there was 59-year-old A.P., who lived thirty miles away in Fort Lauderdale and received a similar package from her doctor. "At first I was startled and confused," she said. "Why would they suggest I take Prozac Weekly?"

A. P. didn't realize she was targeted because she took Zoloft, a drug manufactured by one of Lilly's competitors. She had been taking it for panic attacks she suffered as a result of the September 11 terrorist attacks. She didn't think anyone besides her physician knew she suffered from panic attacks and was concerned that this had somehow become public. She said she threw the pills in the garbage disposal and shredded the package. A third woman, J. N., had been taking Prozac but had stopped several years earlier. As she had just applied for life insurance, quite correctly stating that she was not currently being treated for any psychiatric condition, she became fearful the insurer would reject her if it discovered the apparently readily available false information about her.

We didn't know, and ultimately never found out, exactly how wide-spread the free Prozac Weekly effort was. However, Gary and I had evidence the marketing ploy was also being conducted in California, Oregon, and possibly Washington. There is also reason to believe it was practiced in other areas nationwide. According to an Oregon pharmaceutical representative who quit Lilly because of his misgivings about the program, the company's regional sales managers heavily pressured reps to increase sales of Prozac Weekly beginning in the latter part of 2001 and, as far as we knew, continued the campaign. Lilly's ostensible purpose in developing the new weekly formula, it seems, had less to do with convenience for the patient and more to do with extending its patent rights and maintaining Prozac's share of the booming antidepressant market.

The market was about to be inundated by lower-priced generic tablets, and Lilly was expected to lose about 80 percent of its $2.5 billion annual Prozac revenue. The company needed a financial boost. The solution: get its Prozac customers to switch to Prozac Weekly, which was still under patent.

The drug company's plan called for sales representatives to woo doctors with whom they had good relationships and from whom they would receive the names of patients on Prozac and other antidepressants. The representatives would then go to a cooperative pharmacist who would fill the prescriptions and receive reimbursement coupons for their costs from Lilly.

The Prozac Weekly tablets would then be returned to the doctors in patients' names to be distributed the next time they came in. If a patient refused Prozac Weekly, the doctor could simply block out that patient's name and fill in another. Sometimes the representatives would double-up by getting a second Lilly reimbursement coupon to be used for the same patient. It's unclear exactly what doctors gained from participating, but there is indication of Lilly's largesse toward them in the form of perks and promotional incentives—a subject I would repeatedly encounter in my litigation to come.

The drug reps would get bonuses from Lilly for their performance.

Wherever the scheme was carried out, Lilly showed huge spikes in sales of Prozac Weekly, for which it was paying for both the cost of the prescriptions to pharmacies and bonuses to representatives. The Oregon drug rep who quit did so because he believed the scheme was in violation of Lilly's own authorized policies and procedures. Raising the same ethical considerations that we described in our lawsuit, the drug rep said he believed this marketing scheme may have endangered the health of some patients who were switched from another antidepressant to Prozac in apparent violation of FDA rules.

In late 2001, shortly after he learned of the marketing program, the sales rep informed his bosses at the company about what he viewed as Lilly's illicit or illegal practices. The marketing campaign allegedly stopped for a few months but later resumed. When the rep continued to complain, he was told he was not being a team player, which lead to his resignation. His narrative, the important points of which are supported by at least one other Lilly drug rep in Oregon, made it appear that the marketing scheme originated at a regional level and didn't necessarily have the approval of Lilly's corporate headquarters. However, Lilly's head office had to be aware of large increases in Prozac Weekly sales in some areas but not in others.

In the districts where sales were greatest, as its records would have shown, Lilly was not receiving income but was paying out an amount that was commensurate with its increased sales. Either Lilly was incomprehensibly negligent in its oversight of its own employees, or it encouraged the plan because it would show, no matter how falsely, sales growth that would have a positive effect on the company's stock. Lilly may, in fact, have seen its conduct as appropriate. Long before we came along and long before the revelations of the Kentucky trial, Lilly and its competitors in the pharmaceutical industry had been deeply involved in manipulating the welfare of their patients to boost profits. Drug companies had historically paid pharmacies, benefits managers, and doctors in the hopes of switching their patients from a competitor's brand to their own. There are numerous examples of such apparent collusion with doctors and healthcare organizations, which may be illegal under federal statute and, if not illegal, are certainly betrayals of the trust patients put in their physicians. Two specific examples concern whistleblowers who stepped forward much like the Oregon pharmaceutical rep who came to us.

One such whistleblower, who provided information to the U.S. Department of Justice, accused Bayer Corp. of inflating its wholesale costs for certain drugs in order to establish them as the basis for Medicaid reimbursements. Bayer then allegedly offered discounts off the wholesale prices to physicians, which meant doctors would be reimbursed at the phony higher rate and pocket the difference. More prescriptions written meant higher reimbursements and a larger increase in Bayer's share of the market.

Another whistleblower, John Foster, was fired in 1999 from his national account manager position at Warner-Lambert Co.'s Parke-Davis unit allegedly after he complained about $679,000 in cash and other incentives paid to Ochsner Health Plan, a Louisiana-based health maintenance organization. Pfizer, Inc., which purchased Warner-Lambert, settled a lawsuit by the Justice Department in 2002 for $49 million with Foster receiving more than $3 million for his whistleblower role. That year, the drug industry's trade association swore off these practices but only in the form of a "voluntary" code of ethics.

Illicit payments are one reason the costs of prescription drugs have steadily increased at a rate far outpacing inflation. The introduction of new, blockbuster "miracle" drugs, as Prozac was dubbed, involves costly marketing campaigns that push that figure much higher. The great irony is that, unbeknownst to the general public, most new drugs aren't new at all but instead are reformulations of existing chemical compounds that are neither innovative nor lifesaving.

GlaxoSmithKline, for instance, changed the chemical structure of its antidepressant Wellbutrin, creating a "new" product, Wellbutrin XL, which was touted to have new benefits. It was essentially the same drug. The company then noticed that its drug helped smokers quit, so it gained FDA approval to market it as Zyban—same drug, different approved use, more profit. Further, while the pharmaceutical companies go to great lengths to inform the public of the amount of money they spend developing these new drugs—portraying themselves as valiantly waging the war on illness and disease—they don't divulge *how* that money is spent. From my calculations, approximately 30-50 percent of a drug company's budget is spent on advertising. In many cases, a large portion of a new drug's actual development cost—money they claim to be investing in producing the drug—is underwritten by the NIH and other government programs and institutions. Pharmaceutical companies won't reveal that taxpayers are often footing the bill to help develop these drugs, which sadly aren't any safer or more effective and are being sold at inflated prices.

Trying to get patients to switch brands is a more serious issue than just marketplace competition. What we learned in our research into Prozac was that some patients have adverse reactions to it as an antidepressant. Similarly, the antidepressant S.K. was taking could be harmful to someone who is helped by Prozac. The side effects can be minor, but they can also be serious. Neither patients nor doctors need the kind of bait-and-switch tactics Lilly employed for Prozac, nor as we are now seeing, direct-to-consumer drug advertising. Oftentimes, information about potential negative side effects in the advertising is less pronounced than it is on the drug packaging, which carries a black box warning.

Everyone has seen the ads: a tranquil stroll in the forest with singing birds, soft music, and an affectionate companion. The health risks in many ads are often downplayed, and the benefits are touted in such a way as to prompt patients to ask their doctors "if this drug is right" for them.

In addition to the problem of misleading advertising, there's also the literature that accompanies the product and information posted online. As we saw with Prozac and would see with many other drugs, the manufacturers routinely report and publish under the guise of medical literature the positive findings of drug studies, dismissing the disappointing ones and using language that has no practical informational value. The result is that patients in ever-increasing numbers are demanding and receiving prescriptions for medications they don't need and shouldn't be taking.

In all fairness, the ads do mention or refer to possible side effects for certain kinds of patients. But this is accomplished with rapid speech in TV spots and minuscule type in print advertisements. These ads, which must be successful or the companies wouldn't continue to spend billions on them, are problematic in other ways too. Under the influence of advertising, patients have been known to go "doctor shopping" until they find a physician who will write the prescriptions they are looking for. According to the General Accounting Office (GAO) of Congress, an average of nearly 10 million patients today have both requested and received a prescription for a drug after seeing an advertisement for it.

The FDA has promulgated regulations to prevent false or misleading advertising, but it doesn't have the legal authority to pre-approve either the television commercials or the print ads and, in most cases, investigates only when a complaint is made, usually by a competitor. The agency had a limited investigative staff during our litigation of the Prozac Weekly case in 2002. Thus, the likelihood of an advertisement being deceptive was enormous. As of the writing of this book, the FDA appeals to health care professionals and consumers to report misleading ads through its Bad Ad outreach program, which is administered through the agency's Office of Prescription Drug Promotion.

Although companies almost invariably remove or revise the misleading ad when confronted, I've seen occasions when they replace it with one that is more spurious. By the time the FDA gets around to the first complaint, the ad may have already completed its run and done its mischief, and the same is true if questions are raised about the replacement ad. It can typically take as much as 78 days from the initial complaint to the FDA for a letter to be sent to the offending company that lists required changes for the commercial to be in compliance. About a third of all TV pharmaceutical commercials run for only two months or less.[17]

Even so, some companies and their products are repeat offenders.

Over the past decade, GlaxoSmithKline has received as many as 14 letters from the FDA requiring changes in its advertising, Merck & Co. has received five while its Schering Corp. subsidiary has received at least six. In one year alone, the FDA issued four letters to Glaxo, then Glaxo Wellcome, concerning its allergy nasal spray, Flonase, because of unsubstantiated claims and failure to provide information about major side effects. Similarly, the FDA sent four letters to Pfizer regarding its broadcast and print advertising for Lipitor.

As we would find with ads for Prozac Weekly, the characters and settings in many of the pharmaceutical ads deliberately convey benefits that contradict or go much further than the claims made on drug packaging. In at least one instance, it was discovered by the GAO that the camera in the television commercial jumped around to distract the viewer from what the announcer was saying about the drug's negative side effects and the description of those who shouldn't take the medication. It's wise to remember that, despite the horror stories I've been conveying about dangerous pharmaceuticals, most of them do what they claim to do when taken as prescribed.

Though doctors are themselves the frequent victims of misinformation, they are the ones to whom a patient should listen, not the voice of an actor in a television commercial. Only two countries in the world permit direct-to-consumer drug advertising, New Zealand and the U.S. It's shocking, yet true.

In some instances, doctors can be their own worst enemies by their acceptance of what I consider thinly veiled pharmaceutical company bribery. Until recently, the industry flooded healthcare providers with freebies and gifts. Drug sales reps routinely wooed physicians, nurses, and other medical staff with sample products, meals at expensive restaurants, tickets to concerts and sporting events, and "educational" seminars in vacation destinations. Litigation and new laws limiting the practice placed a spotlight on a disturbing trend: the more prescriptions written, the more benefits physicians received.

I have found it goes far beyond just this. As I discovered while litigating a vaccine falsely purporting to prevent Lyme disease, many high-profile trend-setting physicians are covertly on a corporation's payroll or stand to profit handsomely by the successful launch of a new medical product. They accept honorariums, consultancy fees, and research grants in return for favorable endorsements and reviews of pharmaceutical products. Corporate scientists prepare the speeches that seemingly unbiased physicians deliver at medical conferences and ghostwrite the papers they publish in major medical journals. The Physician Payment Sunshine Act that took effect in 2013 requires greater transparency and reporting, much to the chagrin of drug companies who protest it will cost too much to assemble the reports.

If such financial incentives did not pump up sales or compromise a physician's professional judgment, pharmaceutical companies wouldn't have been paying doctors off. Here's the truth: until recently, the practice proved to be highly successful for drug manufacturers who passed the costs on to consumers through the sale of overpriced medicines. As many physicians and experts in the field have told me, if the medical profession stood up to pharmaceutical companies, older or generic drugs would be found to be as effective or even more so than the expensive new ones being marketed.

In just one example, a Harvard study showed that the popular diuretic Warfarin, sold as Coumadin, which is used to combat conditions including blood clots, is at least as effective and safer than newer drugs including Pradaxa and Xarelto. Warfarin has been on the market for more than a decade and costs less than 10 cents each compared with the newer drugs, which are more expensive and come with greater risk.

These kinds of pharmaceutical tactics were on vivid display as we delved further into our Prozac Weekly case, especially the possible quid pro quo relationship that existed between certain doctors in Florida and Lilly. Ultimately, we wouldn't find out whether Holy Cross Hospital or the four signatories to the letter or both were paid by Lilly. S.K. says Dr. Lambert told her the medical group provided signed letterhead for Lilly and allowed the company to draft the content, a practice that was pioneered by debt-collection agencies who sometimes paid public officials to use their stationary.

It's a betrayal by the institutions we place our trust in. Whether or not the medical group members or anyone at the hospital had final approval of the content, we don't know. We also cannot think of any explanation that would be exculpatory. Neither do we know how many people got the "congratulations" letter—whether it was in the hundreds or the thousands—or how many would have received it if S.K. hadn't gone to a lawyer.

We also obtained proof that the database provided to Lilly by doctors to market its new version of Prozac was riddled with errors. This was the case for both 16-year-old M.G. and 59-year-old A.P. They had never taken any antidepressant medication, had never been diagnosed as depressed, and had never had symptoms of depression. This was particularly frightening, as it shows we're at risk of having our private health care information, whether it's correct or not, sold to the highest bidder.

The potential for privacy violations doesn't just end there. Employees at pharmacies and pharmaceutical companies, including data-processing clerks and anyone who happens to pick up the readouts, were able to access our clients' prescription histories or, as with A.P. and M.G., create fiction by cobbling together medical records from a variety of sources. Moreover, based on S.K.'s experience, samples were sent from Walgreens by regular mail, not registered or certified mail, which meant that if the intended recipient had moved, the person now living at the address would get not only the drugs, but also private information about the former tenant or owner. Even more worrisome, if patients gave a business address, the samples would go there, increasing the likelihood that their medical conditions would be revealed to bosses and fellow employees.

Our lawsuit asked for monetary damages to be paid to the members of the class, attorney fees to be paid for by the defendants, and, among other demands, for Lilly and others to be permanently barred from engaging in the alleged scheme. We also demanded the implementation of procedures to assure that confidential prescription information be limited to purposes specifically authorized by members of the class. As we put it in our complaint, the conduct "was so outrageous in character and so extreme in degree as to go beyond all possible bounds of decency and can be regarded only as atrocious and utterly intolerable by a civilized society."

While we were waiting for the case to be heard—justice was moving especially slowly in our lawsuit—there was troubling news of Eli Lilly's influence in Washington, DC. Big Pharma's robber barons were apparently in action again, only this time they seemed to be on steroids.

The event was the signing of the Homeland Security Act, which President Bush hailed as an "historic action" that demonstrated "the resolve of this great nation to defend our freedom, our security, and our way of life."[18] No explanation was given for why, buried in this massive bill, there was a provision that would protect Eli Lilly from lawsuits by parents whose children had been harmed by impurities found in its vaccines. Could the inclusion of this "get out of jail free" clause have been a result of Bush having appointed Lilly's Sidney Taurel to a seat on the Homeland Security Advisory Council?

As Gary Farmer likes to say, sometimes our government moves like a race car and sometimes like a cruise ship. In the case of our Prozac Weekly litigation, the courts moved at a snail's pace. And with each passing day, sales of Prozac accumulated. On May 16, 2005, almost three years after we filed our suit, Judge Robert Andrews in Broward County dismissed the case in a 14-page decision in favor of the defendants. The judge ruled that he could find "no disclosure of plaintiffs' confidential and private medical information to anyone other than those authorized to receive that information."

Think about this for a minute. Communications between a patient and a physician are confidential and a patient's personal medical records are also confidential. But the court declared that pharmaceutical sales representatives were within their rights to obtain such information and act on it as they saw fit, without permission from patients. Not only was this the incredible judgment—a classic case of a corporation's rights trumping an individual's—but in subsequent years, this practice has been further sanctioned by our courts. It's now even automated! The information is readily accessible by the Big Pharma reps via an internet download.

In this way, and without permission from physicians, drug manufacturers can find out which doctors are prescribing specific drugs and whether or not patients are filling those prescriptions. The drug companies know details of consumers' medical conditions and lab tests, and in some cases their ages, income, and ethnic backgrounds—all on the alleged basis that drug reps and the manufacturers they represent can be sure the "right" drugs are given to the "right" patients.[19,20] Conversely, legitimate scientific researchers and physicians cannot consult pharmaceutical company records or review clinical trial data to find out whether the "right" drug is really the wrong drug. In whose interest have these measures been put into place?

We lost this case, but we were far from allowing Lilly to get away with what we believed to be flagrant disregard for patients' rights. We would target the company again, armed with documents that proved what we had previously only suspected.

STEPHEN A. SHELLER

CHAPTER 3: THE "CURE" MAY BE THE PROBLEM

S.K. in Broward County was not the only one who got the Walgreens mailing for Prozac, but she got angry and called an attorney about it. Others followed S.K.'s lead. Among them was a group of Lilly sales representatives, some of whom were pharmacists, who saw me interviewed on television about our Prozac case. They were troubled by what I had to say and felt compelled to expose pharmaceutical industry fraud that was beyond even what I had imagined possible. Gary Farmer and I, joined by attorney Michael Freedland from Gary's office, would ultimately work with the whistleblowers for nearly a decade. The first of several new cases that came as a result was Lilly's illegal marketing of the drug Zyprexa, an antipsychotic that accounted for nearly a third of the company's revenue in 2003, with worldwide sales totaling near $40 billion.

What's important to understand about Zyprexa is its incredible financial performance, though it has dubious success as a safe and effective medical treatment. This isn't the paradox it first appears to be. Former *New England Journal of Medicine* (NEJM) editor Marcia Angell described the process succinctly:

Suppose you are a big pharmaceutical company. You make a drug that is approved for a very limited use...How could you turn it into a blockbuster...You could simply market the drug for unapproved ("off-label") uses—despite the fact that doing so is illegal. You do that by carrying out "research" that falls way below the standard required for FDA approval, then "educating" doctors about any favorable results. That way, you could circumvent the law. You could say you were not marketing for unapproved uses; you were merely disseminating the results of research to doctors—who can legally prescribe a drug for any use. But it would be bogus education about bogus research. It would really be marketing.[21]

This, we would discover, was exactly what Lilly had done with Zyprexa and had likely done earlier with Prozac. One of the many problems with this type of fraud is that prescription drugs can cause more problems than the condition or disease that they're designed to treat. Moreover, the negative side effects of one prescription can send patients to consult their doctors about the "new" condition, only to be prescribed yet another drug that can produce still more negative side effects.

At the risk of sounding alarmist, let me share a statistic: the negative side effects from drugs send approximately 4.5 million Americans to the doctor's office or the emergency room each year—far more than for common conditions such as infection, strep throat, or pneumonia.[22] These reactions are, according to the National Academy of Sciences, Engineering, and Medicine's Institute of Medicine, the fourth leading cause of hospital deaths, topped only by heart disease, cancer, and stroke.[23]

If that doesn't frighten you, maybe this will: researchers at the Indiana University School of Medicine used a computer program to analyze 5,600 drug labels and more than five hundred thousand labeled effects. The study found, on average, a "mind-numbing" seventy potential negative drug reactions for each drug studied. The most commonly prescribed drugs averaged around one hundred side effects each, with some drugs containing as many as 525 listed reactions.[24] As should come as no surprise, medications typically used by psychiatrists and neurologists have the most complex potential drug reactions and side effects. Some are garden variety, like vomiting, anxiety, arrhythmia, irregular or fast heartbeat, difficulty swallowing or breathing, seizures, fever, or persistent sweating. Some can be disabling and permanent: diabetes, dystonia (movement disorder), neuroleptic syndrome (neurologic disorder), shaky leg syndrome, tardive dyskinesia (frightening involuntary body movements and tics), hypogonadism (low testosterone), and, as we've mentioned, suicidal ideation and "a desire to kill."

Negative side effects aside, it gets worse. The "success" of one drug spawns other drugs. Because of Prozac's and then Zyprexa's meteoric success, along came other atypical or second-generation antipsychotics, with each competing company developing a version of their own: Geodon (Parke-Davis/Pfizer), Seroquel (AstraZeneca), Abilify (Bristol-Myers Squibb), Invega and Risperdal (Johnson & Johnson/Janssen), and others. Although far more expensive than Thorazine, Haldol, and Perphenazine, and the first generation of antipsychotics they replaced, their attraction was based on the widely held perception in the medical community that they were safer to use and could thus be prescribed more widely. At least this is what the marketing departments of drug companies declared.

Whether these drugs are actually safer or more effective is a much-debated point, and I'll not argue the pros and cons except to say that both generations of drugs are said to work in essentially the same way: by blocking dopamine and serotonin receptors in the brain to reduce manic and delusional behavior. They do not cure the underlying conditions they are prescribed for but effectively mask the symptoms. This can be beneficial when an out-of-control patient must be chemically restrained, but problematic in the long term, as patients and physicians can be lulled into believing that the underlying condition has improved when this isn't the case. The important difference is that psychiatric wards were the primary domain of Thorazine and Haldol, while prescriptions for Zyprexa and its near cousins are filled most commonly at your local pharmacy.

From a marketing point of view, the timing was right for an atypical antipsychotic feeding frenzy. Patents for Big Pharma's star hitters, SSRIs and antidepressants, were near running out. What would fill the void? The rise of these new psychotropic drugs was a potential gold mine. Predictably, an intense competition among manufacturers ensued, putting pressure on sales reps whose managers demanded or at least tacitly approved of them bending the rules. They were aware that doctors were allowed to prescribe drugs off-label (meaning, as I've said, for uses not approved by the FDA) but it was, and is, a criminal violation to market these drugs to physicians for off-label uses. It is one thing to prescribe a drug off-label when it is completely necessary—when there are no alternatives and someone could suffer grave injury to his or her health. But that was not the case for most of the prescriptions being written for Zyprexa and most of the antipsychotics. Big Pharma management's attitude was that if you couldn't or wouldn't aggressively push doctors to prescribe these drugs off-label, you needed to look for another line of work.

Based almost exclusively on questionable Eli Lilly–funded testing, the FDA approved Zyprexa in 1996 for the short-term treatment of schizophrenia, and in 2000 for the long-term treatment of schizophrenia and bipolar and manic disorders. Zyprexa quickly became the industry's best-selling antipsychotic and Lilly's first billion-dollar drug. As is the case with so many other pharmaceuticals approved for one condition and used for another, Zyprexa was heavily prescribed off-label, most notably for depression, anxiety, and panic attacks. This practice was so popular that psychiatrists eventually began recommending it for children and teens whom they determined were crying too often, suffered from insomnia, or had trouble concentrating at work or in school. Unbelievable but still true, a cousin of this drug would eventually be recommended for "compulsive shopping disorder."[25]

Did we learn nothing from off-label marketing in the past? I am reminded, in this regard, of my litigation over DES, a synthetic estrogen, which was promoted off-label in the 1950s, 1960s and into the beginning of the 1970s to hundreds of thousands of women with menstrual problems, morning sickness, infertility, and even something described as "excess height disorder." So popular was DES that some companies were even adding it to vitamin tablets! The tragedy is that it didn't help a single one of the prescribed or off-label conditions, and its side effects included cancer and reproductive abnormalities that were passed from one generation to the next.

Zyprexa's off-label uses were also questioned. Powerful as the drug was as a mood stabilizer, patients began reporting a wide range of negative side effects, most notably excessive sleep, rapid weight gain, diabetes and diabetic precursor conditions such as hyperglycemia (high blood sugar), pancreatitis in which the pancreas shuts down, sexual dysfunction, and tardive dyskinesia, a disorder resulting in involuntary, repetitive Parkinson's-like symptoms such as nervous twitches and uncontrollable tics. The truly insidious thing about such negative side effects is that even if you stop taking the drugs, there are many instances when the condition it has caused cannot be cured, and the longer you take the drug, the more likely you are to develop the problems. If I haven't frightened you yet, this may: when used long term, Zyprexa and other so-called second-generation atypical antipsychotics may induce or increase the likelihood of psychotic behavior and suicide because it's thought to shrink the frontal lobe of the brain. As Dr. Nancy Andreasen, the former editor-in-chief of the *American Journal of Psychiatry*, reported, the more of these drugs a patient ingests, the more brain tissue is lost and the greater the cognitive impairment. By solving one problem for a period of time, others were likely to appear.[26] The truth of the matter is that many psychotropic drugs create a rebound effect that mimics the condition that was the basis for the original prescription, thereby creating an endless loop of symptoms, creating the perpetual patient or client.[27] Children prescribed an antipsychotic to help control their behavior might, over time, find themselves with chronic mental illnesses.

The bad news about Zyprexa became public in 2001, despite heavy lobbying by Lilly. In November, the *Journal of the American Medical Association*, the FDA's Center for Drug Evaluation and Research, and a prominent Duke University Medical Center physician linked Zyprexa with hyperglycemia in adolescents. FDA committee members subsequently published a report in December in *The American Journal of Medicine* linking Zyprexa to diabetes. The following year, British and Japanese researchers reported similar side effects, and finally, in 2003, the FDA demanded that Zyprexa carry a black-box warning, the strongest warning label possible for prescription drugs. With the new warning came new litigation. As a result of the publicity about the new black-box warning, individuals who developed diabetes started filing lawsuits all over the United States. Those lawsuits began in 2003 and 2004. Having already taken a major pharmaceutical company to court, I was hesitant to join what could have become a stampede of Zyprexa cases. There were too many challenges, not the least of which was the fact that Lilly was one of the largest and most influential drug companies in the world and, as we had seen with the Homeland Security Act, had paid confederates at all levels of the government and its regulatory agencies.

What promised to be an equally great obstacle was the large body of research and testing that Eli Lilly paid to have done on Zyprexa and the articles it had sponsored or ghostwritten; those materials had achieved the level of medical consensus and were used by the courts to determine what the jury could hear and what it could not. In other words, I wouldn't be able to introduce evidence and testimony if it contradicted what Lilly declared the facts to be. Difficult as this may be to believe, and contradictory to what you see on television courtroom dramas, it's the reality and warrants explanation.

The 1923 *Frye v. United States* ruling permits the introduction of scientific evidence only if it has "general acceptance" in the relevant scientific community. The *Daubert v. Merrell Dow* ruling, which came seventy years later, permits scientific evidence to be introduced in court if it meets the judge's standards for reliability. Thus, if a pharmaceutical company can publish enough peer-reviewed journal articles claiming its products are safe, expert testimony cannot be presented to the contrary. Never mind that the pharmaceutical companies themselves invariably write these articles, pay physician to put their names on them, and use financial inducements to encourage journal editors to publish them.

To describe the matter as simply as possible, if the Frye rule had been around in Galileo's time, his assertion that the world was round would not have been admitted in court because it was contrary to the scientific consensus of his day. Under Daubert, Galileo might get his day in court, but only if the judge decided his scientific studies followed the then-accepted research methods that had already proven the earth was flat.

Herein lies a major challenge in going after corporations as big as Lilly in today's legal climate. A corporate defendant can spend hundreds of millions of dollars to pay for clinical trials, research studies, and journal articles that influence what a judge will use to determine what constitutes the medical consensus. Plaintiffs, on the other hand, don't have the funds to conduct their own drug trials or underwrite research that may be favorable to their cases. They are also greatly limited by what expert witnesses they can call upon to testify on their behalf. Unless their expert witnesses have adhered to the methodology and practices of their consensus peers, they will be barred from addressing juries. They cannot challenge the status quo unless they are members of the status quo to a degree.

Yet another challenge we faced with Zyprexa litigation was the labeling on the pill bottles, which listed the negative side effects alleged by plaintiffs. The defendants could and would argue that they had never made a secret of what could happen when taking the drug. This is precisely why ever-increasing lists of negative side effects in ever-smaller print are included with prescription purchases. The purpose is not only to warn the user of the negative side effects, but to also try and build a legal firewall to keep from being sued.

Finally, there was the added difficulty of proving that the most pronounced Zyprexa side effect, diabetes, was an actual result of taking the drug. Research as far back as the 1920s noted a connection between schizophrenia and diabetes, and more recent testing showed that schizophrenics developed diabetes at a rate four times higher than that of the general population, regardless of whether they used antipsychotic drugs. Proving the connection to Zyprexa could be a time-consuming and very expensive proposition.

Gary Farmer and I were weighing the pros and cons of taking Lilly back to court and how we might overcome these obstacles when we spoke at length with sales rep James Wetta and other current and former Lilly drug sales reps who had helped us with our Prozac Weekly case. They hadn't shed much new light on how Lilly marketed Prozac, but what they had to say about the Zyprexa marketing scheme came as a revelation.

CHAPTER 4: WHISTLEBLOWERS SPEAK UP

Studies have revealed that over half of all Americans have witnessed or been pressured to commit wrongdoing at their workplaces.[28] They are nurses who have observed medical malpractice, salesmen who have been advised to lie about product safety or reliability, accountants who have discovered financial fraud, teachers who have been pressured to inflate student test scores, and lab technicians who have been told to suppress negative test results. Examples are too numerous to tally. Yet the number of people willing to step forward to expose these betrayals are remarkably few. The most conservative estimates place that number at less than 2 percent. Less than 1 percent actually put their livelihoods on the line to come forward. James Wetta and several of his current and former Lilly colleagues are among them.

Wetta, a 36-year-old husband and father, had worked as a drug rep for other pharmaceutical companies before joining Eli Lilly in 2000, where he specialized in Central Nervous System (CNS) drugs. During his tenure, there was an important change in how these drugs were being marketed. Though Zyprexa had once been promoted to psychiatrists by a dedicated CNS specialty sales force, it was being widely marketed to primary care practitioners for issues that weren't approved by the FDA or listed in the Zyprexa package insert. The sales team Wetta joined, for example, was dedicated to selling the drug off-label to the non-schizophrenic elderly for symptoms commonly associated with Alzheimer's disease and dementia. Profits were the motivation, not patient safety.

Most important for our case, Wetta maintained that Lilly had failed to give patients and physicians adequate warning of Zyprexa's negative side effects. It did this by submitting misleading information to the FDA and distorting and burying disclaimers in fine print. Lilly had also boosted drug sales by arranging with physicians and caregivers to switch patients' medications without their approval or knowledge. And this was just the beginning of even more egregious conduct.

Lilly sales reps, Wetta said, targeted mental patients who were too medicated to reasonably know what drugs were being given to them. He said that Lilly had also purposefully designed its marketing campaign to include children too young to be diagnosed as suffering from acute mania. Children in the foster care system were also mentioned specifically, as this subgroup didn't necessarily have guardians who were in a position to supervise what medications were being given to their children. When Wetta complained to Lilly's marketing director about these sales tactics in 2002, he was told to either join the program or look for another job.

We learned from the whistleblowers that such treatment is typical of the pharmaceutical industry. Rather than dialogue with an employee or provide workers a forum where concerns can be safely expressed, employers routinely stifle criticism. The employee becomes marginalized and suspect in the eyes of co-workers until he or she chooses to quit. This was the case with Wetta. After two years of complaining about shady sales tactics, he packed his things and took a job selling real estate.

Fellow salesman Robert Rudolph also left Lilly, only he had been with the company for decades. One of the things that offended him the most was how sales reps were allowed into doctors' offices on weekends to collect names of patients taking certain drugs in hopes of switching them to Lilly products. "I was put in a position of breaking the law, in my view, or quitting," he told us.

Rudolph approached another Lilly sales rep, Hector Rosado, who in turn contacted others. They didn't just have stories to tell; they also had documents to back up their claims. Among the most damning were reports of drug trials that linked Zyprexa to suicide. In five pre-marketing clinical trials conducted by Lilly involving 2,500 patients, 12 patients committed suicide, making Zyprexa the drug with the highest suicide rate of any antipsychotic in clinical history. As one of our expert witnesses would later testify, Lilly suppressed data on suicidal acts from these trials and thus increased the likelihood that the drug would be prescribed to at-risk children.

Sadly, many of the documents that I have personally examined—documents showing how Lilly manipulated test results and spun the data—cannot be made public to this day, as they are deemed confidential and are still under court seal. The penalty for breaching confidentiality can mean jail time or a heavy fine. This was the experience of clinical drug trial reviewer Dr. David Egilman, a clinical professor of family medicine at Brown University. Driven by a desire to reveal important health information contained in the Zyprexa documents, he leaked several online and was fined $100,000. This was payable, of course, to Eli Lilly.[29]

In court, however, we could and ultimately did use the documents.

Equally important to our case were the personal stories of Wetta and the others. Most shocking was Wetta's claim that he and another drug salesman had been on a specialized, long-term care Lilly task force whose sole purpose was to distribute rebate checks and other perks while extolling the drug's effectiveness for a litany of non-indicated uses, most specifically to sedate elderly nursing home residents exhibiting symptoms of agitation, anxiety, and insomnia.

Literature and sales tools were tailored specifically for this purpose, as was a colorful visual ad showing drowsy and sleeping seniors enjoying their golden years in the tranquility of a well-appointed nursing home. To accompany the glossy brochures, sales reps were provided with pre-approved responses to what the company knew in advance would be difficult selling points. If a psychiatrist asked about the negative side effects of Zyprexa, she was instructed to say that the drug was primarily a mood stabilizer that, if taken in combination with antidepressants to mitigate negative side effects, would bring positive results.

In this way, Lilly reps promoted the use of Lilly's drug in combination with other pharmaceuticals, what the industry refers to as "polypharmacy" or "drug cocktails"—the condition that one drug created could simply and effectively be solved by adding another to the mix. Such a drug cocktail was, as you may remember, what had been prescribed to seven-year-old Gabriel Myers when he took his own life in his foster family's bathroom. One of the bonuses, from the drug manufacturer's perspective, is that by mixing the pharmaceuticals, it makes it more difficult for a judge and jury to determine which of the drugs caused injury or death.

Using these and other sales tools, a dangerous and powerful antipsychotic was promoted to people for whom the drug had no other health benefit than as a sleep aid but had the potential side effects of diminishing mental capacity and increasing risk of diabetes, heart attack, and seizure. The overall message to sales reps was "Push the drug and change the prescription, and bonuses are yours." Patients were not informed of the financial incentives of their physicians or care providers for changing or adding to their prescriptions, and some patients were never told that they were actually being given the drug.

Those brochure ads of seniors enjoying the tranquility of their golden years couldn't have been further from the truth considering how this drug and so many other antipsychotics were often being used: as a chemical restraint, a convenient tool for nursing home staff or others entrusted with eldercare. "Five at five" was the Zyprexa sales pitch: five milligrams dispensed at 5:00 p.m. would keep a patient quiet all evening.

At $10 a pill, the return for Lilly was astronomical. Zyprexa brought in an estimated $400 million in new revenue and a 40 percent gain in new sales attributed directly to off-label usage. It was impossible for Gary and I to calculate the human toll in the number of damaged lives, even without factoring in those patients who legitimately needed to be treated with the drug and became diabetic or suffered from diabetic-related complications or pancreatitis. Even more insidious, as the whistleblowers told us, was that while Lilly had been misrepresenting Zyprexa's risk of causing weight gain, suspecting it contributed to diabetes, the company had enjoyed prominent sales of its insulin drugs. In other words, Zyprexa-related weight gain ostensibly boosted other Lilly drug sales.

To what lengths would the company go to protect its market share?

The answer to that question was evident in the experience of

Kentucky Medicaid prescribers in 2002. Because Zyprexa cost approximately twice that of similar drugs and showed little evidence of being superior to its competitors, state prescribers decided to exclude it from their preferred list of drugs. To their shock and embarrassment, the nonprofit National Alliance for the Mentally Ill (NAMI) spoke out against the decision, placed full-page ads in newspapers, barraged state officials with letters, called for hearings, and bused protesters to those hearings.[30] Unprepared for such a show of force, officials quickly reinstated Zyprexa on the preferred pharmaceuticals list.

What was not revealed until the following year was that the entire NAMI campaign—including newspaper ads, a letter-writing campaign, and busloads of protesters—was paid for by Lilly. NAMI was funded to the tune of $11.7 million by drug companies, and Lilly was the largest donor. The drug company's largesse included loaning NAMI a Lilly executive who worked at NAMI headquarters and whose salary was paid for by the company.[31]

As investigative journalist Ken Silverstein would write, deceit was the name of the game. Here was a trendsetting and influential mental health nonprofit whose grass roots were being watered by Lilly's millions.

CHAPTER 5: INDICTING BIG PHARMA

Based on what Wetta and the others shared with Gary and me, I decided to forgo what had become the accepted model in pharmaceutical litigation: gather as many clients as one could and then prove the drug had unreasonably harmed them. Rather, I wanted to show how one pharmaceutical company had wantonly committed fraud on hundreds of thousands, perhaps millions, of its customers. It had actively and purposefully engaged in a nationwide campaign to sell Zyprexa to a class of people for whom its drug was unapproved. The company had minimized and misrepresented the drug's dangers and placed profits above public safety. Further, if we convinced judge and jury of how one company conducted business, perhaps the entire industry would come under scrutiny.

With exposure as our goal, we decided to try a litigation strategy driven by lessons I had learned taking on the tobacco industry a decade earlier. Previous attempts to beat the tobacco giants in court had failed primarily because plaintiffs could not prove that smoking alone caused cancer, and even if it did, "buyer beware" warning labels made it a moot point. The ill or injured knew what risks they were taking—or such was the claim.

I adopted a radically different approach when I filed my tobacco company litigation. After several false starts and in conjunction with other attorneys bringing suit, I went after the tobacco companies on the grounds of fraud. My aim was to prove that so-called low-tar, light cigarettes were even more dangerous than regular cigarettes and the cigarette companies knew it. We also chose not to take the cigarette manufacturers on single-handedly but to partner with the US government or, more precisely, forty-six of the fifty states as co-plaintiffs.

Partnering with the government had made perfect sense. This is because taxpayers pick up so much of the financial burden related to medical conditions brought on by smoking through such programs as Medicaid and Medicare. From a political view, the idea was also a highly attractive one, for by the time I got to court in the mid-1990s, the majority of the public mistrusted cigarette companies. Best of all, from the state's side, the costs of pursuing the litigation were completely underwritten by private counsel—myself and other law firms. Should the private counsel recoup money, the state would keep all returns less our legal fees. This was not exactly an incentive for most attorneys at the time, but it was enough for me. I was passionate about stopping the cigarette companies from selling their poison and, for the first time ever, the tobacco companies were held financially accountable for their lies. The strategy I put in place was then carried on by others and is now being employed overseas to try and rein in the industry.

For our tobacco litigation, we filed class action charges under state consumer fraud statutes. This time around, with our pharmaceutical industry litigation, we utilized a rarely used federal law that dated back to the Civil War. The Federal False Claims Act, also known as the Lincoln Law, was written to impose liability on persons and companies, typically federal contractors, who defrauded government programs by charging outrageous prices or selling inferior products, from horses and blankets to hammers. Similarly, Eli Lilly had harmed the American taxpayer by defrauding Medicare and Medicaid by selling products it knew to be inferior. The concept was a good one, though this would be the first time it would be used to take on a major pharmaceutical company.

Among the False Claims Act's other provisions is a whistleblower clause known as *qui tam*, which is a Latin phrase going back to medieval times meaning "he who sues on behalf of the king." Today, this whistleblower clause allows people who are not working for the government to file actions on behalf of or in partnership with the government. By partnering with the government and filing in this manner, we could not only steer the litigation ourselves, but we could also provide our chief witnesses—James Wetta and our other whistleblowers—with government protections and financial incentives. If we were successful, Wetta and the others could collect a share of whatever settlement or penalty might be imposed on Lilly.

The downside of the plan was that our firm would have to shoulder the expense of preparing and taking the case to court and, if we lost, might be out several hundred thousand or perhaps even a million dollars. It was quite a risk to take considering that the lion's share of any settlement would naturally go to the American taxpayer, on whose behalf we were bringing suit. Moreover, it was quite a risk for Wetta and the fellow whistleblowers. The moment the court made our case public, they would become pariahs in the corporate world, let alone among their pharmaceutical salesmen friends and colleagues. Nevertheless, we moved ahead with our suit.

My plan from the start was to file in federal court in Philadelphia because the US attorney's office here had particular expertise in health care fraud. Paradoxically, I wouldn't be going to my own state's attorney general because Pennsylvania is not one of the 29 states that has passed a False Claims statute. To find out why our taxpayers (and consumers of prescription drugs in 21 states) would not be eligible to receive such compensation, you would have to ask our Big Pharma-friendly legislature.

Thankfully, the doors at our US attorney's office were open to us. U.S. Attorney for the Eastern District of Pennsylvania and future congressman Pat Meehan, his deputy, Laurie Magid, and assistant U.S. attorney Joseph Trautwein welcomed us into their offices, interviewed Wetta, and examined our documents. They were also outraged by Lilly's behavior and agreed to partner with us.

As our case developed, we teamed up with former assistant Philadelphia district attorney Mike Mustokoff of the Duane Morris law firm. Several years later, U.S. Department of Justice attorneys would take responsibility for pursuing the case, joining with us. Among them were federal prosecutors Virginia A. Gibson and Margaret Hutchinson. With their backing and support, we were also able to avail ourselves of help from the Justice Department and Health and Human Services (HHS) and the Health Care Fraud Prevention and Enforcement Action Team (HEAT). They provided trained personnel to help us investigate our claims and assigned Trautwein to the case.

As part of a False Claims Act prosecution, different departments of the government get involved in the investigation, sometimes including the FBI, health fraud and FDA investigators, the Office of the Inspector General (OIG), and others. Of equal importance is having a federal judge supervising the investigation. And as previously alluded to, under the judge's watch, the complaint is kept under seal as the case is being built. Eventually, a subpoena of materials is requested, which is usually the first time the defendant is put on notice that it is under investigation for civil and/or criminal conduct. Until the subpoena and the grand jury that may follow, the defendant has no knowledge of the content and scope of the investigation. The defendant doesn't know, for example, if there's a whistleblower involved, a False Claims Act allegation, or something else. The seal remains in place, sometimes for years, during the time the government and law firms gather the evidence leading to civil and criminal charges that can ultimately end in criminal indictment and/or civil settlements to resolve the case.

It was while our whistleblower False Claims Act claim was still under seal that I received an unexpected update from Wetta, who by this time had left the real estate business—the California market had collapsed—and had become a salesman for one of Lilly's competitors, pharmaceutical giant AstraZeneca, located in Wilmington, Delaware. As Wetta's identity as a whistleblower was still secret, he had had no trouble finding another job as a drug rep.

"Steve, I can't believe it," he told me. "It's going on here too." Wetta's reference was to the marketing of AstraZeneca's drug Seroquel, another atypical antipsychotic that had become nearly as popular as Zyprexa.

CHAPTER 6: WHEN ONE ANTIDEPRESSANT ISN'T ENOUGH

At this point in my Eli Lilly suit, I was already stretched thin. There were still many witnesses to depose, research to conduct, drug trials to study, and briefs to write. Moreover, the cost of underwriting our litigation with Lilly was costing my firm hundreds of thousands of dollars, with more spending to come. This was money that we would recoup if we won our case, but there was no guarantee that we would. Still, I took the time to hear Wetta out, and I was glad I did.

His story was frighteningly similar to what he had told us about the Lilly sales department. Seroquel, approved by the FDA in 2000 for the treatment of schizophrenia and in 2004 for the short-term treatment of acute manic episodes associated with bipolar disorder, was being heavily marketed for off-label use.

In an effort to reach children, brand managers had gone so far as to discuss creating *Winnie-the-Pooh*-inspired characters of Tigger (bipolar) and Eeyore (depressed) to sell Seroquel and like many other drug companies, produced an array of child-friendly marketing items emblazoned with product logos.[32]

Just as Lilly had done, AstraZeneca had put together specialized sales teams. One team's chief purpose was to market the drug to inmates, soldiers, and the elderly for unapproved uses. The drug was being used in the treatment of Alzheimer's disease, post-traumatic stress disorder, depression, sleeplessness, ADD, and even to help with anger management. When the team identified a psychiatrist who was willing to go the distance with them, the results were spectacular. In one year alone, the top ten Pennsylvania prescribers wrote nearly 19,000 prescriptions for Seroquel, costing Medicaid $3.6 million.

I wasn't going to turn a blind eye to these allegations. Nor was I going to pass off the heavy lifting to another firm. I already had the contacts with state and federal attorneys' offices to file another Federal False Claims Act case, a team of lawyers who were now steeped in the nuances of pharmaceutical litigation, and medical experts who were willing to testify about the dangers of antipsychotic drugs. The same people who were helping us with Zyprexa could help with Seroquel. Never mind that I might go bankrupt while trying to win the case.

With the Zyprexa suit under government seal (meaning Lilly had no idea of what was coming), we once again filed a case with James Wetta as a whistleblower in the matter of AstraZeneca and Seroquel. As in the Zyprexa case, we filed a Federal False Claims Act and charges under the Anti-Kickback Statute. This time, we charged that AstraZeneca had provided illegal remuneration to physicians and caregivers to promote Seroquel. Often $1,000 or more was paid as a bonus for writing more prescriptions for the drug and promoting others to do so as well; they were often given money as paid speakers as well, but the real money was paid for increased prescribing.

The marching orders for the doctors were to target colleagues who did not typically treat schizophrenia or bipolar disorder, such as eldercare, primary care, and pediatric physicians, and those supervising prison inmates and working in veterans' hospitals. The purpose of these consultations was to verbally encourage the unapproved use of Seroquel without the drug company having to make written claims it knew were not true. In other words, it hired a reputable spokesperson to do its dirty work.

We obtained documents through discovery showing that AstraZeneca had knowingly manipulated the ways test results were presented to the public. The company claimed, for instance, that patients taking Seroquel lost weight and were less prone to diabetes than those taking competing drugs such as Zyprexa, Geodon, and Risperdal, when in fact its own studies revealed the opposite: patients on Seroquel gained an average of eleven pounds a year and the drug was directly linked to diabetes. Positive studies were hyped while negative ones were filed away.

"The larger issue is how do we face the outside world when they begin to criticize us for suppressing data," wrote John Tumas, AstraZeneca's publications manager at the time, in an e-mail in 1999. "We must find a way to diminish the negative findings."

We could, in essence, convict AstraZeneca using the company's own words. We could also convincingly show how AstraZeneca's bad behavior had cost the American taxpayers hundreds of millions of dollars each year. Besides the Medicaid and Medicare reimbursements that were still being paid to AstraZeneca, the Pentagon was spending hundreds of millions each year dispensing Seroquel to soldiers fighting in Iraq and Afghanistan. According to the Department of Veterans Affairs, the Pentagon had already spent $850 million on Seroquel, with nearly 100 percent of the prescriptions written for off-label disorders. Moreover, these figures were in addition to what was paid to the Bureau of Prisons on behalf of inmates.

We would file yet another whistleblower/False Claims Act case, this time against pharmaceutical giant Pfizer for the illegal marketing of its drugs Geodon, Bextra, Zyvox, and Lyrica. Thus, in the process of building not one but three major pharmaceutical cases, our firm grew to include several dozen attorneys working on our behalf, many of them in temporary, rented offices. Had I not won major settlements against the tobacco companies and established partnerships with other counsel, our small firm may have gone under. And all of this, you may remember, had grown out of my pro bono association with Gary Farmer during the *Bush v. Gore* 2000 election litigation, which had led us to take on Lilly for its marketing of Prozac Weekly. As I will repeat once again, we don't have to see the larger picture to set the wheels in motion. Merely taking the first step, even if it's against a Goliath, will often trigger events well beyond our imaginations.

I will save the reader from a lengthy recital of the specifics of our new cases here because you've heard the major points already. Pfizer did much the same as Eli Lilly and AstraZeneca, hyping the positive studies of its drugs and burying the negative. Further, Pfizer's marketing teams, one of which was fittingly called "the Sharks," were dedicated to using the same off-label sales practices as those of its competitors. Their marching orders were to "grow share," a phrase used at training meetings meaning to expand beyond the FDA-approved guidelines. Profits were the motivation and patient safety not a consideration.

Pfizer also provided funding to physician spokesmen for the National Alliance for the Mentally Ill to promote Geodon, its atypical antipsychotic, to children. The spokesmen appeared on behalf of the nonprofit without telling their audiences of fellow physicians and concerned families that they were actually on the Pfizer payroll.

The only big difference between Pfizer and its competitors was that Pfizer had been down this road before with its illegal marketing of its painkiller Neurontin. As part of its 2004 settlement, Pfizer had signed a corporate integrity agreement promising never to use such sales tactics again. According to our whistleblowers, Pfizer's behavior hadn't changed except for perhaps becoming more adept at breaking the law and bending the rules. Pfizer illegally paid physicians recruitment bonuses of amounts varying from $250 to $1,000 a day to attend meetings to promote Pfizer drugs, $500 to help another physician "review" a clinical paper supporting a Pfizer position, and $250 to $1,500 a day for travel and meal expenses to attend conferences in luxury hotels, where they could meet and mingle with their colleagues. In one case, Pfizer paid a physician $4,000 a day to use his personal helicopter to go from one off-label marketing event to another.[33] Perpetuating this fraud was deemed by the company to be "the cost of doing business." It seems the pain and injury this drug and others caused was a matter of business as usual too.

I felt a combination of pride, satisfaction, and anxiety when the Justice Department finally unsealed our complaints. To my knowledge, never before had one law firm, and a small one at that, made such an aggressive effort to hold so many multinational pharmaceutical corporations accountable. Nor had any other firm presented such a significant body of evidence to support its claims.

We might have submitted even more evidence had we not decided to move forward when we did. By this time, James Wetta had left AstraZeneca and was about to be hired by Merck, where salesmen may have been operating under the same marching orders. However, like a spy coming in from the cold, Wetta was greatly relieved to finally go public. Not only had he been operating undercover for over half a decade, but his home had also been under surveillance. He was worried for his wife and daughter. The drug companies knew or suspected by this time that an informant was at work; they just didn't know who or how far-reaching the investigation.

Our celebration of what came next was a private one, for the press was not informed of how we built our cases nor were they introduced to the attorneys who did the actual work. Instead, the Justice Department held the press conferences and took all the credit. The only exception was a brief thank you to my office in our suit against Lilly from Assistant U.S. Attorney Charlene K. Fullmer, who would go on to partner with us in our next major case. She now supervises and prosecutes healthcare and fraud matters as Deputy Chief for Affirmative Litigation in the Civil Division of the United States Attorney's Office in Philadelphia.

In January of 2009, Lilly pleaded guilty to illegally marketing Zyprexa and, by previous agreement, settled civil suits for $1.42 billion, the largest amount ever paid by any one defendant at that time and the largest single drug settlement in US history. The amount included a $600 million criminal penalty for pleading guilty to a misdemeanor. This remarkable record only stood for eight months, until Pfizer too decided to settle, this time to the tune of $2.3 billion. This figure included $1.3 billion in criminal penalties, which set a record. Early the following year, our AstraZeneca/Seroquel case settled for $520 million. In all, we were instrumental in recovering over $4 billion in just a few years. But even these figures would pale in comparison to what was coming next—taking on America's undisputed pharmaceutical kingpin: Johnson & Johnson.

CHAPTER 7: EXPOSING THE BETRAYAL

When I began my career, I could never have imagined that a firm I headed would win three consecutive record-breaking pharmaceutical whistleblower cases. I was justifiably proud of the accomplishment, but still had to ask myself if our litigation had actually changed pharmaceutical companies' behavior.

The settlements we won temporarily lowered the market shares of three giant drug producers and put several billion dollars back into federal and state treasuries, yet none of the corporate officers who put their companies into jeopardy were held personally accountable. Executives were not asked to return the millions of dollars in bonuses and stock options they'd received, and none were charged with criminal behavior. And though these companies were forced to sign corporate integrity agreements, our experience with Pfizer—and again later with AstraZeneca—had taught us that such agreements weren't enforced. It was a Pyrrhic victory, a single battle won in the midst of a war we were losing.

All of the major drugs we had focused upon—Zyprexa, Seroquel, Zyvox, and Geodon—are still on the market. I would try once again to take on a pharmaceutical giant in court, this time to exact justice beyond a monetary settlement. Most importantly, I wanted to expose the depth of the betrayal: from the executives who wrote the marketing playbook to the pandering physicians, media conglomerates, and other paid allies who marketed the drugs. Maybe I could also upset the FDA's partnerships with those corporations they were charged, but failed, to regulate.

Foremost on my radar was Johnson & Johnson, whom we knew had fraudulently marketed its blockbuster antipsychotic Risperdal off-label to non-schizophrenics. Not only had our whistleblower drug reps told us about J&J's off-label marketing schemes, but former J&J employees had also agreed to act as expert witnesses. The challenge would be in framing our case in such a way as to expose the greater picture of how J&J, the world's largest healthcare company, and its Janssen subsidiary, the maker of Risperdal and Invega, had gained off-label market share. Drug reps took their marching orders from the top.

Among the active and former J&J drug reps to speak to us was Victoria Starr, who is as fine and brave a young woman as I've had the pleasure to represent. A second-generation pharmacist with a degree from Washington State University, Vicki began her career as an Eli Lilly sales rep based in Portland, Oregon. She made the jump to J&J's Janssen subsidiary in 2001, where, at age 30, she believed she would make greater use of her extensive pharmacology expertise.

Quick to laugh as she is to cry, Vicki had a rude awakening when she entered the Janssen training program. She was not expected to sell Risperdal using technical arguments. Rather, she was encouraged to make generalizations that would induce pediatricians and others to prescribe the drug off-label. Risperdal, she was to tell prescribers, could be used to calm upset children. Physicians had only to lower the adult dosage. Never mind that the drug hadn't been approved for children and that no studies, to her knowledge, had been conducted. "Marketing to kids was the priority," she said. "That was where the company saw the future growth."

Surprise turned to concern when doctors began complaining to Starr about some of the negative side effects their patients were experiencing.

Among those side effects was extreme weight gain. Patients would put on as much as a hundred pounds in a matter of months. This was especially alarming because the number of negative side-effects being reported were not reflected in the sales literature. There was a disconnect between what Starr was seeing in the field and what the company was telling her.

When Starr raised questions with her superiors, she was told to downplay the issues. She was also provided with sales brochures, which she could leave behind with physicians. These sales materials didn't focus on schizophrenia—which was what the drug had been intended to treat. The emphasis was on using it off-label to treat a "full spectrum" of symptoms that included just about all mental health conditions. Among the photos on these brochures was that of a young girl playing a violin, what drug reps later referred to as the "Yo-Yo Ma" brochure. This image, and others, suggested that the most high-functioning child could safely use the drug without mental impairment.

After two years selling Risperdal and seeing the children of family friends as young as three being put on the medication, she had had enough. Upset, she called Hector Rosado, a friend from her days with Eli Lilly. Unbeknown to Vicki at the time, Rosado was working with us on our Zyprexa case. Rather than helping her get a job at Lilly, which had been her intention, he recommended that she become one of our *qui tam* whistleblowers. "Call Sheller," he told her.

What a story Starr had to share with us! In the days and months to come, our confidence in what she had to tell us about J&J's marketing to children and other sales practices only increased, and would later be reinforced when we eventually received, through the discovery process, subpoenaed pharmaceutical company brochures, interoffice strategy memos, and office manuals. Along with her testimony, these materials would go a long way toward making our case. This, however, was just the start of her work for us. After she had finally had enough of J&J, and in early 2004 quit her job, she once again encountered the dark side of the pharmaceutical giant.

While working in a senior position with a company managing nursing home pharmacies in the Portland area, and waiting, like James Wetta before her, for government prosecutors to make public our *qui tam* suit, she was repeatedly approached to prescribe the drug to seniors suffering from anxiety and dementia. Forget about the high-functioning school-girl with the violin. J&J was now pitching Risperdal as cost effective. This was because nursing home labor costs could be reduced by keeping patients in a Risperdal chemical straight-jacket. "They will sleep all night," the drug reps told her, failing to emphasize, of course, potential negative side effects that included death, diminished mental capacity, and increased risk of diabetes, heart attack, and seizure.

Not long into her new job, Starr was invited to a three-day eldercare seminar in San Francisco in which J&J was sponsoring an informational breakfast devoted to using Risperdal. She didn't just attend the breakfast on our behalf to take notes. With help from federal agents she wore a remote transmitter under her blouse and recorded what was said.

Despite fears that she would be caught, and how her many friends and colleagues in the pharmaceutical industry might later view her actions, she eventually became the key witness and named plaintiff in our *qui tam* Risperdal suit, which we filed in April 2004. "I had to do what was morally right," she told us. "My conscience wouldn't let me do otherwise."

Among other reps to come on board as our case developed was Judy Doetterl, who had worked for J&J for three years. She, like Starr, was tasked with selling Risperdal off-label. She too wore a hidden transmitter to record marketing presentations.

In addition to sales reps, one of J&J's regional business directors, Kurtis J. Barry, also joined our whistleblower team. What would make his testimony so important was his executive position in the J&J hierarchy; from 1996 to 2009 he was the Risperdal product director and oversaw 60 sales reps and six managers. There was no question, so far as Barry was concerned, who orchestrated the marketing schemes. "The decision to market, promote and sell Risperdal for off-label purposes to the elderly population was made affirmatively and deliberately by defendants' executive and management personnel, and carried out under their authority and direction," he told us.

One of our highest profile witnesses to come forward in the personal injury cases was Tone Jones, the former Oklahoma State quarterback, who had signed on with Janssen in 1998 and eventually became a marketing executive. Among the many other things he had to tell us about Risperdal marketing practices were the inducements that J&J paid to physicians to prescribe the drug to children from 1998 through 2006. Inducements included cash kickbacks, along with a full range of marketing promotions such as all-expenses-paid trips to golfing resorts, admittance to seminars, and meals at exclusive restaurants.

Jones also added items to our list of prescriber inducements that at first seemed the stuff of a Hollywood parody, but proved to be true: drinks at strip clubs, promotional giveaways such as bags of microwave popcorn and brightly colored play toys sporting the Risperdal logo. I expected such incentives from J&J's competitors, but these practices were shameless in that J&J wasn't only in the pharmaceutical business; J&J had earned its century-old reputation selling Band-Aids, baby shampoo, talcum powder, and beauty products.

STEPHEN A. SHELLER

CHAPTER 8: THE BOY WHO GREW BREASTS

In August of 2005, young A.C. came to see me. He and his parents swore to me that Risperdal had made him grow breasts. He wasn't referring to a modestly enlarged bustline but adult female D-cups. More than several hundred children and men would tell me the same thing. Others would grow only one large breast, creating an even more uncomfortable social stigma. In many cases, their breasts would express milk similar to women after giving birth. As insurance defined their condition as cosmetic and didn't cover the mastectomy, only the fortunate few whose parents had enough money could have the unwanted breasts removed. But even then, there were several cases when the removed breasts began growing back before the surgical wounds had even healed. It was as if the victims' brains and hormones had been permanently rewired.

I don't know what horrified me the most, that a drug commonly prescribed for attention deficit disorders and behavioral conditions marked by anger and irritability could disfigure a young boy already struggling to fit in or that children were exposed to this possible side effect by a drug that there was no legitimate reason for them to be taking in the first place. Did J&J's simply forget its famous credo "to put the needs and well-being of the people we serve first?" Crafted in 1943 by Robert Wood Johnson, a member of the company's founding family, the Credo, the company says, is more than just its moral compass. The company owes its first responsibility to the mothers and fathers, doctors, nurses, and patients who use its products. Based on what I was seeing, I went looking for information connecting Risperdal with increased breast growth. Buried in small print on page seventeen of the Risperdal package insert under "Adverse Reactions" and the heading "Use in Special Populations," I found a single word in a very long list of disclosed potential negative side effects: gynecomastia. In more than three decades of reading lengthy lists of possible side effects, I hadn't before encountered the word and had to consult my medical dictionary to make the connection. Gynecomastia means abnormal breast growth in males (and sometimes females as well) and is attributed, among other things, to increased levels of the hormone prolactin, which helps women produce milk after childbirth.

If I didn't know the definition of gynecomastia, I would have no reason to believe that parents of children prescribed Risperdal knew what it meant either. My guess was that the vast majority hadn't even read the insert and instead relied on their physicians to tell them what side effects they might encounter when taking the drug. Further, I suspected that the reason gynecomastia wasn't featured more prominently as a side effect in Risperdal's literature was that the drug's effects were more masked in children than in adults. The condition may slip by unnoticed. As it was, the warning that was listed fell under the category of "Special Population," never mind the fact that children and young adults represented the largest proportion of Risperdal's "Special Population" off-label users. The company warned about weight gain but failed to mention that boys and young men could develop breasts and wind up needing bras or having a mastectomy. They were the ones whose lives would seriously change because of Risperdal. The labeling was also a problem for prescribing physicians. A doctor reading the product insert would have no reason for concern about gynecomastia because the insert listed the condition as a "clinically irrelevant" (meaning less than one in one thousand) and rare side effect. In other words, breast growth was considered so rare that a risk aversion couldn't be calculated. This wasn't, however, what I was seeing by the number of boys coming into my office. I only had to call a few physicians to connect Risperdal with gynecomastia in a clinically significant way. Surely someone in the pharmaceutical behemoth that was J&J had noticed too.

The more people I interviewed, the more upset I became. As I would discover, the nightmare for young gynecomastia sufferers is both physical and psychological. It can begin with taunting on the playground at school. You know the kind: "He's got girl boobs!" or

"The fairy queen needs a bra!" This inevitably leads to withdrawal from the public, and for boys going through puberty, it invariably results in gender crises. They start looking more like their mothers than their fathers. Most young boys can't understand what's happening to them. In several notable cases I investigated, adolescents took their own lives. Parents too suffered shame as they blamed themselves for allowing their children to take the drug and, in instances when they could not afford cosmetic liposuction or a mastectomy, were powerless to help.

At the very least, the entire family was traumatized. This was the case of my clients Philip and Benita Pledger and their son, Austin. They asked me to use their names in my book, so their personal story might become a lesson to others. One of the reasons is because their son, Austin, is autistic. His challenges began years before his mother and father had ever heard of Risperdal. The Pledgers are from a small town in rural Alabama and live in a double-wide trailer. They had been trying to have children for twelve years and were considering adoption when Austin, their miracle child, was born. By the time Austin celebrated his second birthday, it was clear that he was autistic. He avoided making eye contact and he failed to pick up on the facial expressions of others. Gradually, other challenges came along. Periodically throughout the day, he would suddenly clap his hands and shout or fly into a rage and beat his head on a table or the floor. Occasionally, he would pinch or bite himself or whomever was closest to him. But despite these hurdles, he was able to attend school and live a relatively normal life. This was made possible by the care and attention he was given by his parents, teachers, classmates, and the greater community of concerned and loving people around Austin. They were his extended family.

Risperdal was prescribed at the recommendation of a University of Alabama neurologist when Austin was seven years old. The physician thought it could help. Though the drug was only approved for treating symptoms of schizophrenia in adults, the physician believed it would soon be approved for other uses and could be especially helpful for autistic children. At least, this is what he had been told by Janssen drug reps, who it was later revealed had visited his office 20 or more times over a two-year period. No mention was made of gynecomastia. Nor was there a black-box warning on the label. Benita and her husband had no idea that taking a mood-stabilizing pill could possibly cause their son to grow breasts.

Philip and Benita were hesitant to put Austin on Risperdal or any other drug because their situation was manageable. However, if medication could safely help to calm Austin, it would be easier for everyone. "I had never given him any medicine before," Benita, an extremely caring parent and intelligent woman, told us. "So, I was nervous about it. I wanted as much information as I could get."

Besides reading the Risperdal package insert, she called Janssen's 1-800 telephone number to discuss her son's condition and what giving him the drug might do. She got an answering machine and, several weeks later, a form letter that failed to address any of her specific questions.

Risperdal seemed to help, but it wasn't the panacea that she and her husband had hoped for. Austin still had emotional eruptions; they just weren't as frequent as they were before taking the drug. Instead of eight to 10 daily outbursts, he would have four or five. The problem the Pledgers encountered was their son's incredible weight gain, which began in second grade when he had been on the drug for a mere two-and-a-half months. By the end of third grade, he had put on nearly 50 pounds. And it was this weight-gain that initially kept family members from noticing what was happening to his chest. He was growing breasts.

Rather than taking him off the drug—the Pledgers and their physician still had no idea that Risperdal might have been causing the breast growth—their neurologist added Topamax to what became a three-times-a-day drug cocktail. Topamax, a Janssen anticonvulsant approved for epilepsy, was then widely being prescribed off-label for migraines. Drug reps were also pushing it in combination with Risperdal because it allegedly counteracted the weight gain. Other drugs too, which would include Geodon, Abilify, and Prozac, would later be added to the mix in an effort to discover the combination that would be most effective. What Benita wasn't being told was that each new prescription came with still more side effects.

Austin's condition continued to get worse. He would eventually weigh 300 pounds and his breasts became 46DD cups. Understandably, Austin was embarrassed. Benita would often catch Austin looking in the mirror and then crossing his arms in front of his chest and attempting to press his breasts down. As the Pledgers' friends would report, this caring mother, who never cried because her son was autistic, was frequently in tears because of the anguish Austin felt concerning how he looked and at the confusion and disappointment he felt for looking different from other boys and men. On one occasion, when an insensitive teacher mentioned his large breasts in front of him, he smashed them with his hands into the desktop. For Austin, continuing at school was out of the question so Benita quit her job to take care of him. A child already trying to come to grips with the fact that he was somehow different from others was now truly even more different in just about every way.

This, however, was not all. Austin's gynecomastia was permanent.

CHAPTER 9: FOLLOWING THE MONEY

Long before we filed suit on behalf of the Pledgers, we knew that J&J had resorted to Lilly and AstraZeneca's playbook when it came to the media campaigns it used to sell its drugs. Excerpta Medica, a medical communications agency serving the pharmaceutical industry, had been hired by J&J to ghostwrite and present its pharmaceutical drugs in the best possible light and would also be named in our lawsuit. The company had been paid to saturate medical journals with positive stories heralding the release of Risperdal, which, in my opinion, was little more than advertising to push the drug off-label. More than 20 articles appeared in psychiatric journals and medical publications touting Risperdal as the equal of all the new atypical antipsychotics. Physicians took notice and, as J&J's message reached the mainstream media, so did parents of at-risk children.

Even the *New York Times* went on record in Risperdal's support when it quoted Janssen's clinical research director, Richard Meibach, as claiming that the drug had "no major side effects," understating the dangers of this drug.[34] As the *Washington Post* reported, the drug supposedly didn't cause sleepiness, blurred vision, impaired memory, muscle stiffness, or the many negative side effects commonly associated with the previous generation of antipsychotics. The fact that it might cause diabetes, manic behavior leading to suicide, and the myriad of other conditions we knew came hand in hand with the other atypical antipsychotics was not referenced on the label but buried in small print on the package insert. In one advertisement, which Janssen ran in the *American Journal of Psychiatry*, the company went so far as to claim the drug was as harmless as a placebo.[35]

We also knew, or at least suspected, that the drug studies J&J had used to win FDA approval were rigged, just as we had seen when other dangerous drugs had sped through the approval process. The 1993 study that won approval for Risperdal compared multiple low doses of the drug with a single high dose of Haldol, the previous generation's antipsychotic. By lowering the intended dosage of Risperdal and upping the normal dosage of Haldol, J&J could be relatively certain of Risperdal's having a good safety profile in comparison. Even the FDA's reviewers, we were told, noted that J&J's studies were incapable of providing any meaningful comparison of the two drugs, and according to one of our whistleblowers, the FDA had specifically warned J&J not to make claims that its drug was any more effective or superior to its predecessor. Yet the FDA granted approval and fast-tracked Risperdal onto the market.

Was the FDA being managed like the doctors had been? Were we seeing hard evidence of the Big Pharma alumni club in action? We had only to look more closely at FDA records and then follow the money to unravel the truth.

Though the agency's stated goal in this new era of "reform" was to streamline the regulatory process to make it more efficient, rigorous, and transparent, the deliberations over Risperdal were carried out in private, without disclosure of scientific data or a public discussion. All we know for certain, from the official record, was that on April 19, 2004, the FDA sent a warning letter to Janssen. In the agency's own words, Janssen "misleadingly omits material information about Risperdal, minimizes potentially fatal risks associated with the drug, and claims superior safety…without adequate substantiation."[36] From what we were told, no credible evidence of a clinical benefit had ever actually been presented to the FDA by independent, non-industry generated studies to offset what we assumed was evidence of the debilitating and disabling adverse effects of all atypical antipsychotics. Now, it seemed even more outrageous that the FDA approved the drug.

Careful review of the documents brought much more to our attention. Most curiously, the FDA had issued the Risperdal marketing license *after* the company withdrew its application in England, where the agency's British counterpart had determined that safety problems necessitated strengthening restrictions before conditional approval for short-term treatment of manic behaviors could be granted. The drug didn't win pediatric approval in Canada for similar reasons.

Shouldn't those concerns have compelled the FDA to be especially conservative and cautious before proceeding? Serious questions were also raised about the FDA's 2006 decision to approve Risperdal for autistic children for whom the drug would have little or no obvious benefit except to reduce aggressive tendencies by drugging them to sleep or impairing their mental processes to the point where they acted as if they were asleep. Common sense told us the drug might have profound negative side effects.

Risperdal's success obviously had nothing to do with efficacy but with consensus building and what we soon learned were very well-paid psychiatrists. According to our whistleblowers, foremost among them was Dr. Joseph Biederman, a name we were, sadly, all too familiar with. His research had sanctioned the dosing of millions of children with powerful, adult psychotropic drugs. Among those were seven-year-old Gabriel Myers, four-year-old Rebecca Riley, and toddler Destiny Hager. Biederman, a Harvard medical professor and Massachusetts General Hospital researcher, was ranked as the scientist with the most-cited ADHD research in the world.[37] He led studies examining the prevalence of bipolar disorders in children and almost single-handedly redefined the practice of classifying all mental disorders in children. He did this by conducting studies that purported to show that a substantial minority of children diagnosed with ADHD actually had pediatric bipolar disorder.

In one much heralded study, Biederman reported that nearly a quarter of the children he treated for ADHD also met his criteria for bipolar disorder and should, therefore, be prescribed antipsychotics. Prior to his study, such a diagnosis was only reserved for older teens and adults who had undergone periods of depression interspersed with dramatic episodes of manic behavior. Biederman changed the playing field by offering a definition of bipolar behavior that consisted entirely of irritability and mood swings, which in essence gave psychiatrists license to treat virtually all children with antipsychotics.

Hence, when it came to prescribing these drugs, the line between Bipolar I and Bipolar II became blurred, despite significant medical differences. All patients seemingly became eligible to take the drugs, and the results speak for themselves. Between 1994 and 2003, pediatric bipolar diagnoses went up 4,000 percent in this country.[38]

Thanks to Biederman, many conditions could conceivably fall under the broad canopy of bipolar behavior, including depression, ADHD, and ADD—these are diagnoses I very well could have qualified for in my youth if such conditions had been given a name back then. One of the latest additions to the diagnostic lexicon is oppositional defiant disorder or ODD, which describes youths who often argue with adults, lose their tempers, and are angry, resentful, and easily annoyed by others. What this new diagnosis did, in essence, was to turbocharge what can only be described as Pharmageddon.

I knew about Biederman from our previous suits, but we weren't aware of the degree to which he was on the Big Pharma payroll. Few of his colleagues or anyone beside the pharmaceutical executives did. We discovered that between 2000 and 2007, he had received as much as $1.6 million in speaking and consulting fees for promoting drugs to treat the same disorders that he could be credited personally for redefining. He had failed to report this outside income to Harvard. Moreover, J&J paid Biederman $700,000 to underwrite a research center that was devoted to testing and promoting Risperdal. Based on our extensive investigations, we deduced that he had helped J&J coordinate a massive informational program that won the support of thousands of fellow child psychiatrists.

I would have enjoyed cross-examining Biederman on the witness stand. Thanks in no small part to what we uncovered about his ties to J&J, a U.S. Senate investigation got there before me and revealed that Biederman's consulting arrangement was the tip of the iceberg when it came to conflicts of interest in medicine.[39] Rather than being embarrassed, Biederman arrogantly lauded the service he was doing for child psychiatry. He compared his work on bipolar disorder to such scientific breakthroughs as the first vaccinations and castigated his critics by saying they weren't on his esteemed level.

When questioned by a colleague of mine on this point, Biederman recited his credentials, highlighting his status as a full professor at Harvard.

My colleague then asked him what, if anything, was on a higher level than a fully accredited Harvard medical professor. Biederman declared, in no uncertain terms, "God."[40]

The appearance of so much questionable activity, along with the company's deep pockets, made J&J an obvious target for litigation, and the initial wave of suits focused, as we expected, on claims that J&J hid or misrepresented studies showing that Risperdal caused diabetes, affected sexual development, and had other negative side effects. I knew better than anyone else that a strong case could be made along these lines, but I was also certain that by focusing on conditions such as diabetes, J&J would argue, truthfully, that people with bipolar and other manic disorders were more likely to suffer from diabetes than the general population. Proving that an individual's condition was a result of the drugs would be extremely difficult.

One of the things I couldn't understand was why J&J's marketing arm had tried so hard to convince physicians that Risperdal was no better or worse than any of the other antipsychotics on the market. Janssen's 2003 marketing plan had actually stated as fact that Risperdal was the same as the other antipsychotics. This was a curious thing to put in a sales plan considering that every drug company I had encountered so far claimed that its product was better than its competitors' or, at the least, stood out because of its value for the cost. This might seem a rather insignificant point but, for someone so steeped in the finer points of pharmaceutical company misbehavior, it gave me pause. Why had J&J and Janssen actively pursued a multimillion-dollar marketing campaign to downplay what made its drug different?

Risperdal's effect on the bodies of young men who had used the drug would later make the answer abundantly clear.

1 Philadelphia police hold local black panthers at gun point in the early 1970s following what a judge later rule was an illegal raid on their headquarters. Then a young civil rights lawyer, Sheller went to court to seek their release.

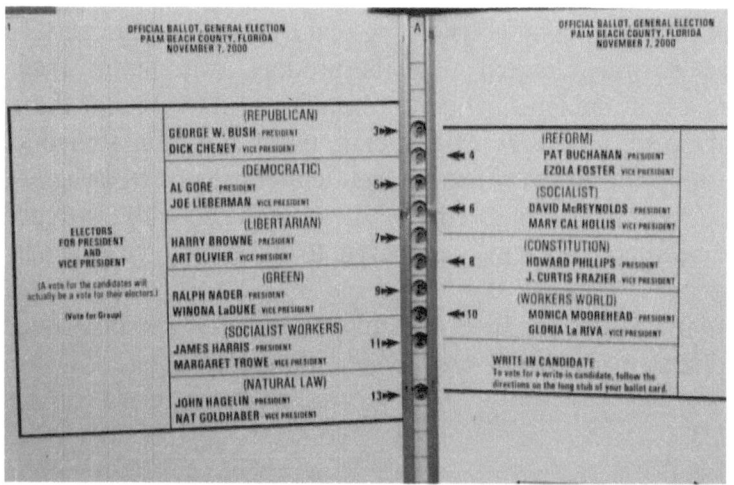

2 The infamous butterfly ballot's confusing design was blamed for thousands of miscast votes in Broward County, Fla. in the 2000 election pitting George W. Bush against Al Gore. Sheller led a team of Democratic Party lawyers seeking to overturn the results.

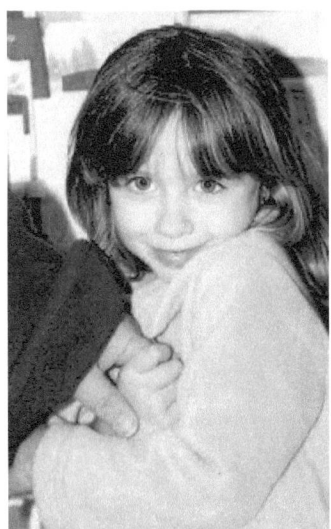

3 Three-year-old Destiny Hager from Council Grove, Kansas died from taking Seroquel, Geodon, and Risperdal among other powerful adult antipsychotics prescribed to children with attention deficit disorders. Most children's deaths from psychiatric drugs go unreported.

5 The tragic case of Gabriel illustrates much of what is wrong with the overuse of powerful antipsychotics to treat behavioral problems in children. In 2009, Myers, then seven years old, hung himself in the bathroom of his suburban Florida foster home after being prescribed a powerful cocktail of mood stabilizing drugs.

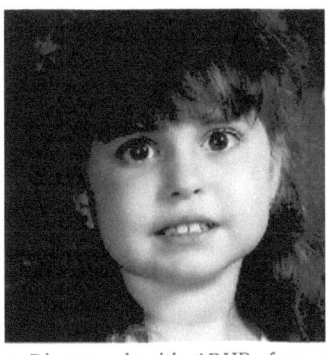

4 Diagnosed with ADHD, four-year-old Rebecca Riley died of an overdose of antipsychotics Seroquel and Depakote in her Massachusetts home. Her preschool teachers reported that she appeared to be so medicated that she needed help ascending stairs and sitting in her chair.

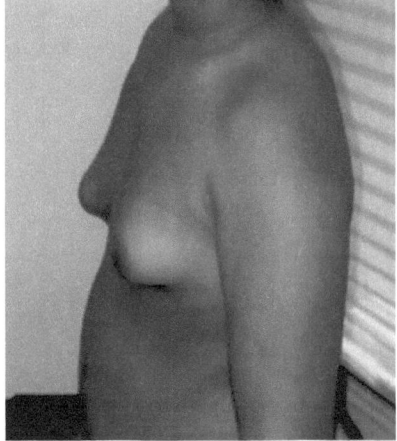

6 Risperdal, a powerful second-generation anti-psychotic, has been implicated in the growth of female breast tissue in males.

7 Alex Gorsky is chairman of the board and chief executive officer of Johnson & Johnson. He served as vice president of marketing at Janssen, a J&J subsidiary, when it had ramped up Risperdal sales to children.

8 Sheller interviewed by then CNN correspondent Greta Van Susteren during the Florida vote recount following the 2000 presidential election between Democrat Al Gore and Republican George W. Bush.

BIG PHARMA, BIG GREED

9 Sheller with consumer advocate Ralph Nader at a conference on direct to consumer advertising by pharmaceutical companies. Sheller has been a vocal critic of the practice, arguing that the television ads often are highly misleading and stimulate consumer demand for drugs they often do not need.

10 For a time, Janssen representatives engaged in the off-label marketing of Risperdal to physicians treating children. One of the marketing ploys was to distribute Risperdal Lego blocks to physician offices.

CHAPTER 10: RISPERDAL AND THE DOWNSTREAM EFFECTS

Taking on J&J over its marketing of Risperdal was by no means a new idea as we had already set the example with our pioneering whistleblower litigation with Lilly and AstraZeneca. You might say we had helped to create a cottage industry that had now become the main event in pharmaceutical litigation. As a result, many other attorneys were considering litigation with J&J, and several firms had already filed injury suits. I too would be filing injury suits, in addition to our *qui tam* whistleblower litigation claiming Medicaid and Medicare fraud. However, there were several important legal questions I had to answer before launching a major civil action: How frequently did Risperdal actually result in gynecomastia? How much did J&J and its Janssen subsidiary know and when did they know it?

Based on what we'd discovered, I put the now-considerable resources of our firm into representing more than a hundred civil suits brought on behalf of injured children and their families. As I'm still trying many of these cases and taking new clients on an almost daily basis, I can only reveal the aspects of our evidence that appeared in public disclosures in cases that have already been settled or where the judge has permitted evidence to be made public.

The vast majority of the evidence we collected was obtained through the discovery process and came directly out of J&J's and Janssen's corporate files along with the records of pharmaceutical industry ghostwriter company Excerpta Medica. This material consisted of about 22 million pages of correspondence and reports—what's called a "document dump." It's a way that many corporate litigants have of turning over the required documents while obfuscating the truth in an avalanche of irrelevant paperwork. Finding the incriminating evidence was a task that took our team of attorneys and paralegals more than three years. We found more than enough to accomplish what I had set out to do: link corporate executives to a marketing plan to sell a dangerous drug to children—those who stood the most to lose by taking it.

How do I begin to describe the depth of J&J's deceit? My files contain several hundred horror stories of children similar to Austin Pledger who were maimed or disfigured. But the real substance of our case rests in J&J's awareness that this might happen.

Even before drug trials began with human beings, years before Risperdal's release, J&J scientists were reporting that risperidone, the active ingredient of Risperdal and Invega, was causing unusual mammary gland stimulation in rats and dogs. The pharmacological effects were the same in all doses; nerve receptors in the brain were triggering unusually high levels of prolactin. As Risperdal didn't appear to cause other significant negative effects, researchers decided to see what happened in human trials.

The results in human trials were similar to those in the animal studies.

After taking a single dose of Risperdal, the volunteers showed prolactin levels increased by 500 to 1,000 percent. Though only short-term testing was done and with few volunteers, one of the test subjects developed a full-blown case of gynecomastia. The scientists conducting the experiment reported this to J&J and debated whether to withdraw the patient from the study. J&J executives responded in writing by saying that due to raised levels of prolactin, such an outcome was possible, but they didn't think gynecomastia was sufficient reason to remove the volunteer from the study. In other words, years before the drug's actual release, J&J admitted that there was a relationship between Risperdal and gynecomastia. J&J had seen it for itself. The company also presumably didn't inform the patient or his physician, though this would have been the morally correct action to take. It's also important that executives were made aware that gynecomastia didn't appear to be a negative side effect of the other atypical antipsychotics on the market. Risperdal was somehow different.

A now-public internal memo exchanged between J&J executives while Risperdal was still in clinical trials attests to this, but in a different context:

"Prolactin elevation with Risperdal has received particular attention due to its receptor-binding affinities. These are different from other atypical antipsychotic agents and can lead to sustained elevated prolactin levels. Symptoms...include gynecomastia," it reads.

What was the extent of the risk to potential Risperdal users? J&J didn't list gynecomastia as a potential negative side effect on its original package insert in 1993. This came later, in 2003, when J&J admitted that it was a risk but claimed that the condition was so rare that it couldn't even attach an adverse reaction number to the condition. Internal memos between sales reps and the J&J marketing department, however, revealed what wasn't on the packaging.

A training document for sales reps stated that there was a 1 percent risk of developing gynecomastia. The label itself said "rare" (and remarkably, so does today's label), which is one in a thousand. So, the training manual was contrary to what was listed on the labeling. Even this, however, turned out to be a falsehood, as an internal document indicated the real incidence was between 5 and 10 percent.

As we studied the documentation further, we discovered that executives were telling overseas drug regulators what they weren't even telling their own sales reps: regulators were told that the chances of contracting gynecomastia were 4.6 percent. An internal company memo between executives showed the figure to be 6.1 percent, and one of J&J's own studies, which the company did not make public but did show its own sales reps, put the figure at 12.5 percent. If this figure is correct, it means that approximately one or more in every ten males and females exposed to Risperdal could conceivably suffer abnormal breast growth.

This was a serious problem, and the company knew it, which is logically why J&J created a confidential Global Prolactin Task Force.

This team of executives and sales reps was led by seasoned drug-marketing guru Gahan Pandina, who was working diligently to understand J&J's liability, what he referred to in correspondence as the "Risperdal, prolactin, and downstream effects." In other words, he was charged with finding out how much the company stood to lose in lawsuits if it kept the drug on the market. There was no forthcoming record from J&J covering this discussion nor whether an actual dollar amount had been arrived upon. All that could be concluded from the documents we received was that J&J took a proactive approach.

They weren't going to remove the drug from the market but, instead, attempt to steer a course around it.

A 2001 training manual instructed sales reps to lie about the dangers of prolactin increases in the body. They were specifically told to say that changing prolactin levels in the human body was neither good nor bad. The *2003 Risperdal Business Plan* laid out the strategy in greater detail. Under "Promotional Key Issues," the first goal was to show a "lack of differentiation" between Risperdal and J&J's competitors' antipsychotics. In other words, J&J wanted to show that Risperdal was no more dangerous than the other drugs. The plan was to distract prescribing physicians from the real danger while simultaneously feeding them misinformation.

J&J stated this boldly in yet another document that encouraged sales reps to "minimize the risk and importance of prolactin." The goal was to get physicians to believe that (1) Risperdal didn't increase prolactin any more than its competitors, and (2) oh, by the way, prolactin doesn't matter much anyway. Both, in my opinion, were huge lies.

J&J executives also went out of their way to discourage doctors from monitoring the prolactin level in their patients' bloodstreams because it might shed light on what Risperdal was doing.

Unfortunately for Risperdal users, J&J went even further than failing to monitor a problem it was well aware of. In an undated internal document entitled "Now Is the Time to Grow Your Risperdal Market Share," sales reps were instructed to tell prescribers that all of the atypical antipsychotics increase prolactin in the same amount; no one knows whether increased prolactin is good or bad; and that, if there were any concerns, they should add a second drug to a patient's daily antipsychotic cocktail. Remember three-year-old Destiny Hager? She died after taking a combination of Risperdal and eight other drugs.

Such egregious behavior makes one wonder about what other potential side effects prescribers were not told about. As a recent Drexel University study on SSRIs has shown, there may be a link between Risperdal and autism.[41] Another study, which has not been made public, is purported to allege that Risperdal and other drugs commonly prescribed to children with ADD and ADHD shrink the brain.[42] How many more horrendous side effects will be discovered?

There was no question that doctors, nurses, and scientists studying Risperdal had alerted J&J executives to the prolactin problem. This is clear in internal memos and also from a lengthy paper trail of dissatisfied customers, among them a nurse who wrote the following letter to J&J in 2001:

"I am working in an adolescent residential treatment center. We give a lot of Risperdal for aggressive behaviors. While we have been pleased with the decreased negative behaviors, we are seeing a major problem of gynecomastia in the males and lactation among the females because of the increased prolactin levels. Do you have any research regarding this side effect? If taken off Risperdal, will the breasts return to normal size or is this permanent? How high does the prolactin levels have to be before breast development is seen? This is very distressing to the clients, and they are refusing to take the med because of this major side effect...We would appreciate any information or suggestions."

This nurse, who had nothing but the best interests of her patients in mind, simply wanted to know what research J&J had on this condition and whether it was permanent. These were questions J&J did not want to answer. They failed to respond the first time she wrote, or two years later, when she wrote a second letter after learning that J&J sales reps were telling physicians that increased prolactin was nothing to worry about because it was not clinically relevant.

The nurse knew better and so did an upset J&J employee who saw the writing on the wall and wrote, "It seems clear we need to more aggressively own up to prolactin elevation. It's no longer enough to say 'prolactin elevation is not clinically relevant.'"

J&J didn't address the issue except to continue obfuscating the truth. When discussions began about establishing a prolactin help line to handle the growing concerns in the medical community, J&J marketing executive Ronald Kalmeijer told his staff that doing so wouldn't help its bottom line: "Our standpoint is that prolactin-related side effects is a nonissue. Our tactics need to be supportive of that." In follow-up correspondence, he again revealed what was worrying him: "I am not comfortable with sharing so much negative details…I am not comfortable with stating that patients with prolactin-related side effects may benefit from switching [to another drug]."

J&J didn't just kill the hotline; it actively prevented physicians from learning the truth. When a new study showing increased prolactin levels was to be presented at a medical conference, J&J sent executive orders to effectively spin the data. "There are some figures that I think should be deleted," J&J executive Ramy Mahmoud wrote to a physician in charge of preparing the materials for the conference.

Mahmoud got the anticipated response. "I attempted to include only positive data, so that the data cannot be used against us," the physician responded. "I am happy to delete any figures. I am also happy to change any text." When the National Institute of Mental Health planned a study to compare antipsychotic drugs, one of J&J's senior executives told his colleagues, "I think we have to take this very seriously and capitalize on our knowledge of both Risperdal and competitors, trying to influence as much as we can the protocols in order to be sure we get good results."

When child psychiatrist Dr. Eric Benjamin informed J&J about a Risperdal study he had conducted at Phoenix Children's Hospital, J&J immediately offered help "as to how the study should be written up." Its enthusiasm disappeared when the company received Dr. Benjamin's data on prolactin. Of the thirty-five patients studied, twenty-two gained between five and fifty pounds. The response from Janssen's chief executive said it all: "I would prefer NOT TO TOUCH THIS." For reasons that were not clarified in follow-up correspondence, Dr. Benjamin's study never saw the light of day.

Concern over prolactin increase, however, didn't prevent J&J

from flooding the media with upbeat reports. Just as Eli Lilly, AstraZeneca, and Pfizer had done, J&J turned to Excerpta Medica to praise the benefits of their drug. J&J's stated goal, as presented in internal correspondence, was to "redefine how we achieve support for messaging through publications and thereby achieve greater commercial success in the marketplace." Excerpta Medica was paid to "manage the content, direction, and timing of data dissemination to competitive advantage." Before these allegedly impartial articles were even written and the physicians found to affix their names to them as the supposed authors, the contents and objectives of the articles were outlined and the text written by J&J marketing executives.

Where did J&J want its Risperdal articles published? As other documents attested, it wanted Excerpta Medica–generated stories to appear in the publication that would most bolster sales to children: The *Journal of the American Academy of Child and Adolescent Psychiatry*—despite the fact that Risperdal had never been approved for use in children.

Excerpta Medica's program was successful. In 2001, journals highlighted Risperdal more than all other drugs combined. By 2003, half of all Risperdal prescriptions were being written for children and the elderly, and 90 percent of those prescriptions were for vague, hard-to-define, and over-diagnosed behavioral conditions like ADD and ADHD, along with mood disorders, such as depression. J&J studiously tracked these sales yet made no effort to inform or warn prescribers of Risperdal's unique dangers.

During the thirteen years that Risperdal was not approved for children, while Dr. Biederman and others were breaking down the diagnostic barriers, J&J made more than $100 million per year selling its drug to children. It made $122 million in sales in 1999 and $178 million in sales in 2000. Still, J&J wanted more. Its plan was to expand sales until Risperdal became its first billion-dollar seller, which it did, peaking at $4.5 billion in 2007, then $3.4 billion in 2008. By 2010, when the drug's patent ran out and it was competing with generic drug makers, the revenue had dropped to $527 million, according to J&J's earnings reports.

Internal memos outlined the scheme to increase market share to children. First, they would produce a drug that was administered more easily to youth. Initially produced as an injection or an unpleasant-tasting risperidone solution, the drug was reconfigured as an easy-to-swallow tablet called Quicksolv. In conceiving the new product, J&J advisors wanted to make certain that the tablet tasted good and that managed care insurers would cover the anticipated prescriptions' cost. These were the two primary concerns when Quicksolv went into production. "I cannot wait for this to come out," one Risperdal-prescribing physician wrote. "We will give this to every kid [in our hospital]."

In anticipation of Quicksolv's release, J&J pumped out publicity for the drug by posting messages for children and adolescents in abstracts, posters, presentations, symposia, and more journal articles. In one of the most morally reprehensible campaigns J&J launched entitled "Consequences for Not Treating Children," it warned physicians about what may happen if they didn't prescribe Risperdal to children with behavioral disorders. The document suggested that these children could go on to develop or experience antisocial personality disorder, alcohol and drug abuse, anxiety, depression, hospitalization, and criminal behavior that included but was not limited to driving while intoxicated and committing violent crimes.

Dr. Biederman was once again called into action. By this time, the challenge was no longer selling Risperdal to children. J&J had already succeeded in doing that. It was obtaining FDA approval for conditions it was already being prescribed for; in other words, increased sales were not the objective. Rather, for new indications or conditions J&J received FDA approval for, its patent could be extended by an additional six months or a year.

Dr. Biederman stepped up his campaign by working aggressively to convince the FDA that Risperdal was safe and effective, and he used his J&J-sponsored research center at Harvard to prove it. However, to be effective, he had to hide his conflict of interest. In one of the documents we uncovered, a J&J executive acknowledged his pleasure at having Biederman on board, noting that he was "not perceived to be aligned with any [pharmaceutical] company in particular" and that his relationship with J&J demonstrated "a clear example of the utility of partnering...[with physicians who have a significant impact upon the field of child and adolescent psychiatry]."

As internal memos also revealed, J&J helped to write the studies that Dr. Biederman presented as his own, though we might never have known if Biederman hadn't taken the trouble to thank J&J's task leader: "Thanks Gahan...If you could help draft the abstract for Tuesday, it will be great."

J&J's tactics were working. By 2005, Risperdal had become J&J's top-selling product, not only raising the company's stock price but also garnering bonuses for its executives. Meanwhile, thousands and perhaps tens of thousands of children and adults were suffering because of it.

As the minutes of an FDA Pediatric Advisory Committee panel meeting makes clear, over 30 people died from taking the drug in 2007, at least 11 of whom were children whose Risperdal treatment was unapproved by the FDA. Among them was a nine-year-old girl who had suffered a fatal stroke 12 days after starting Risperdal therapy. Now I fully understand that killing someone with a prescription pill is not the same as killing someone with a bullet, but the end result is the same. Had this advisory committee lost sight of the fact that this drug was not approved for children, or was this business as usual at the FDA?

There were no figures made available to the FDA about how many boys suffered gynecomastia, as purportedly no authoritative studies had been conducted. However, as we now know, at least one study had been conducted, but Janssen researchers had lied about its findings and further misled or coerced reviewers of their research data into presenting a false public record of what was actually known about the drug.

Even without this vital information, however, the subject of widespread pediatric use of Risperdal caught the attention of the FDA committee tasked to monitor such trends. Nearly 400,000 children were being treated with Risperdal and over half these children were 12 years old or younger. Adult use was declining by 5 percent while pediatric prescriptions were increasing by 10 percent.

As the session's minutes reported, the committee discussed

adverse events related to product use, off-label use including risks and benefits, age subgroups, product labeling, and the effects of long-term use. Twelve of the 14-member committee concluded that the current labeling was inadequate. Specifically, they unanimously supported labeling in addition to the standard and ongoing safety monitoring.

The advisory committee recommended the following:

"Additional follow-up regarding on-label and off-label product use of this class of drug products with specific attention to age and indication the product is being used for. Additional follow-up regarding metabolic syndrome, growth, sexual maturation, and hyperprolactinemia.

Studies, which may be collaboratively developed with NIH, on long-term effects in the pediatric population of this class of products. Additional follow-up on extrapyramidal side effects in the pediatric population. Additional evaluation of this class of antipsychotic medications and concomitant drug use. Committee is not recommending any public communication before additional discussion that should occur after receipt of data from above recommendations."

Despite these recommendations, no monitoring appears to have taken place, no health studies were commissioned, and no changes were made to Risperdal's labeling. Dr. Thomas Laughren, who had long been a pivotal member of the FDA's Center for Drug Evaluation and Research (CDER) and who sat in on the committee meeting, had apparently overruled the recommendations. He reported that the FDA could do little to fix the problem of off-label marketing, as this was a matter between the physician and the patient. Medical specialty societies, he said, must do the job of educating doctors about the drug's side effects. "It's not the FDA's primary responsibility."

A year later, the Alliance for Human Research Protection reported that Dr. Laughren, like his colleague Biederman, had maintained close, ongoing collaborative ties with pharmaceutical industry officials and industry-financed psychiatrists in academia and professional associations.[43] He had participated in influential industry-sponsored consensus panels convened by the American Academy of Child and Adolescent Psychiatry (AACAP) that had recommended expanded use of atypical antipsychotics for unapproved, off-label uses in children, and lent his name and position to articles for which research and funding were provided by the very pharmaceutical companies whom he was charged with regulating. [44] True to his values, Laughren left the FDA in late 2012 and became a defense expert for drug companies in litigation.

Fortunately, we didn't have to rely on Dr. Laughren's appraisal of Risperdal to build our case against J&J. Former FDA Commissioner David Kessler wrote a 92-page expert report for submission in our suits. Janssen "broke the law," he said. In his own words:

"The promotion of nonapproved uses by a manufacturer, because it undercuts the system and safeguards of drug regulation, is concerning. The promotion of nonapproved uses by a manufacturer of powerful drugs is more concerning. The promotion of nonapproved uses of powerful drugs to the most vulnerable children is most concerning. Janssen's promotion of Risperdal, a powerful drug, for non-approved uses in the most vulnerable children is deeply troubling."

Kessler was not only willing to submit his report for trial, he was also willing to testify as an expert witness. J&J fought the entry of his name onto our witness list at every step of the way, and this was after we added a J&J corporate executive to the same list: Chief Executive William Weldon.

I had the most rock-solid case of my career.

STEPHEN A. SHELLER

CHAPTER 11: BAND-AIDS, BABY SHAMPOO, AND BIG PHARMA

In 2006, after conducting two years of research, we began to file our first 100 individual Risperdal injury cases. As a result of the publicity, more than 1,000 more Risperdal victims would eventually find their way to my office. Interestingly, J&J showed no evidence of willingness to discuss the charges—just the opposite. The company prepared for a protracted court battle, fighting us at every step of the judicial process, from our pretrial discovery requests to the expanding number of executives, marketing reps, and Excerpta Medica consultants we wished to depose.

Four years into our litigation, in September 2010, J&J came under pressure when the jury in a bellwether Risperdal consumer fraud case in Louisiana came back with an astonishing $257 million verdict. We knew with certainty that the case would be appealed and the verdict likely overturned by a higher court, but a precedent had been set. Three months later, a South Carolina judge upheld a $327 million jury verdict against J&J and Janssen for off-label marketing. Though South Carolina's Supreme Court would reduce the penalty to $124 million, another precedent was set.

The trickle of suits—both for side effects such as gynecomastia and for off-label marketing—threatened to become a flood in 2012, when J&J's Weldon unexpectedly announced his retirement. He left with "parting gifts" of $143.5 million in pension, retirement benefits, and deferred compensation. My litigation, and that of other attorneys pressing charges, wasn't cited as the reason, but then again, the press didn't yet know what we and federal prosecutors knew. The paper trail of documents the prosecution was prepared to introduce as evidence exposed the entire chain of J&J command. In what may have been a serious tactical blunder on J&J's part, Weldon was replaced by Alex Gorsky, whose long career with J&J had begun in its Janssen subsidiary. Most important to our cases, he served as vice president of marketing at Janssen when it had ramped up Risperdal sales to children.

From our point of view, the announcement was almost too good to believe. When our primary cases came to trial, we would call none other than Gorsky to the witness stand.

A month after Gorsky's promotion, another state Risperdal case went to trial in Arkansas. In a state with less than 1 percent of the U.S. population, the jury verdict was for $1.1 billion. The media, which had long reported that a total global settlement would be in the neighborhood of $1 billion, had to recalculate. The new estimate was placed at $2.2 billion.

Another case, with our plaintiff, A.B., who suffers from gynecomastia, went to trial in Philadelphia on September 10, 2012, and ended that same day. When we called Gorsky to the witness stand, J&J claimed he was traveling overseas and unavailable to testify. Further, a J&J spokesperson argued, Gorsky had already been deposed for seven hours so his appearance in court was unnecessary.

Travel plans notwithstanding, it was clear J&J's plan was to keep Gorsky off the stand, and a judge agreed he didn't have to testify. J&J attorneys then requested a recess during the trial to discuss a settlement. Ten days later, our second Pennsylvania case came to trial and ended the same way.

On October 4, 2012, we settled four more cases. I can't discuss the dollar amounts in these personal injury cases because, at present, these must be kept confidential.

As satisfying as the results of these trials were and continue to be, nothing could beat the clarion call of November, 2013, when U.S. Attorney General Eric Holder announced that J&J had agreed to an historic $2.2 billion settlement with the U.S. attorney's office in Philadelphia over claims it marketed Risperdal and Invega off-label and engaged in an illegal kickback scheme over the drugs. The case we had developed and presented to the government almost 10 years earlier finally reached a conclusion.

Here in our midst was the largest pharmaceutical settlement for a single drug in U.S. history. And though it was the federal prosecutors whose faces beamed before national cameras to make the announcement, this was, in essence, our client, our case, and our hard work coming to fruition. It took 10 years, yes, but some things take that much time and are worth waiting for.

Did we win?

From a financial point of view, there is no question that J&J has been hit with a staggering federal penalty—a new all-time high for a single drug marketed by a single company. But this penalty is not as significant as I believe it could or should be. Nor will the penalty stop Big Pharma's addiction to off-label sales and the profits. In recent years, J&J shares have traded at historical highs and company executives are among the highest paid in the industry. As *Forbes* pointed out when the settlement was announced, "the potential of off-label sales may just be too alluring for drug makers to kick their habit."[45]

Remember also, in regards to our *qui tam* case, that my own state of Pennsylvania is not one of the 29 states that has yet passed a False Claims statute. Hence, Pennsylvania (and 21 other states) won't receive any of our $2.2 billion settlement! To my mind, that's not justice. It's not even common sense.

CHAPTER 12: PHARMA'S P'S: POLITICIANS, PHYSICIANS, AND PHARMACISTS

The flaws of the FDA aside for the moment, one of the recurring questions we asked ourselves while investigating Risperdal and many other antipsychotics was how do drug manufacturers get away with what we deemed to be overt criminal behavior. The answer may lie with George W. Bush and that fateful election in 2000. For want of a better term, the public, in my view, has been "Bush-whacked."

This was the substance of testimony from Allen Jones, a whistleblower who came to talk to us in 2005, but who ultimately pursued his own case in state court against J&J. I share his story here because it speaks to the influence that J&J wielded, and still wields, over our government officials.

Jones, a graduate of Penn State University, was working in the Pennsylvania Office of the Inspector General in 2002 when he was asked to investigate the state's chief pharmacist, Steve Fiorello, who was reported to be managing a private bank account where he deposited checks from pharmaceutical manufacturers. Jones confirmed that this was indeed the case: Fiorello was depositing checks from several drug-makers, most notably payments from J&J and its Janssen subsidiary, for traveling and speaking fees, despite the fact that government employees aren't allowed to charge for their services or keep honoraria.

Jones didn't, however, stop his investigation here. After further inquiry, he revealed that money was flowing out of Fiorello's account into another government employee's account, that of the director of the Texas Department of Mental Health and Mental Retardation (this agency has since been reorganized and no longer exists under its previous name). Additionally, J&J and its Janssen subsidiary were paying for state officials to travel the U.S. to promote the Texas Medication Algorithm Project (TMAP).

TMAP was purported to help public health officials diagnose mental illness and match patients with appropriate medications and treatment plans. Previous testing of the program had been much heralded by Bush, then Texas governor, who touted the program as a significant time-and-cost-saving diagnostic tool for state public health officials.

As President, Bush initiated the New Freedom Commission on Mental Health. As an aside, it always intrigued me how the 43rd president would often add the word "freedom" to somehow make some of his more onerous acts and legislative enactments more appealing. Anyway, the commission encouraged all states to use the program and fostered legislation that, if enacted, would make TMAP testing mandatory in public schools, publicly funded hospitals, prisons, and other institutions. Pennsylvania was among the state governments that considered buying into the program, which was how Fiorello figured into the equation. J&J had provided him funds to attend a TMAP sales conference in New Orleans, Louisiana.

Through interviews with physicians and drug reps, Jones discovered that TMAP was an off-label marketing program funded by drug companies to promote their products. Patients filled out a questionnaire that would be fed into the TMAP program, which in turn identified at-risk individuals and recommended a particular drug and treatment plan for them. The sales literature didn't reveal, however, the Trojan horse rooted deep within the program. By signing on to the TMAP program, all patients determined to be at risk were automatically given one of the new atypical antipsychotics, invariably one produced by a company that had helped to fund the program's development and testing. There were no holistic or non-pharmaceutical options. The only flexibility was what drug was to be prescribed.

More insidious still was the way that the drug manufacturers had found to avoid overtly marketing their drugs for unapproved uses. The TMAP program did it for them without drug companies themselves having to make claims contrary to FDA guidelines. An extreme but true example of how the system worked involved a five-year-old girl in a trial TMAP program in a Texas elementary school who was diagnosed as suffering from obsessive compulsive disorder (OCD) and prescribed Risperdal. Her stunned parents demanded to see the questionnaire she had filled out. The behavior that had triggered the diagnosis turned out to be nothing more than a compulsion to tidy her bedroom—a condition that, according to TMAP, mandated her being given a drug for schizophrenia.

Jones followed an ever-widening money trail. TMAP's so-called independent advisors were on the pharmaceutical industry payroll. Among them was Dr. Steven Shon, the medical director of the Texas Department of Mental Health and Mental Retardation (now known by another name after reorganization). He had signed undisclosed consulting agreements with Janssen that had given him nearly $50,000 to promote TMAP to Pennsylvania and other states. It should be noted, given what our team would later discover about J&J's promotional undertakings, that the receipt of an honorarium by a public employee who acts in his official capacity is not a misdemeanor but a felony. Such an exorbitant payment to Shon, and so many others, suggests far more than reimbursements covering out-of-pocket expenses.

When Jones submitted his preliminary report to his superior, he was ordered to stop investigating. "Stay away from the drug companies and stay away from TMAP," he was told. From how high up that order came he didn't know, but his instructions were clear. He was to walk away from the investigation. The payments Fiorello received were described to him as a state-related personnel issue and nothing more.

When Jones refused to turn his back on the case, he was demoted and replaced as lead investigator. In turn, the case became a misdemeanor offense. Fiorello had breached accepted protocol and had to forfeit honorariums paid to him. Meanwhile, Pennsylvania moved ahead in 2003 to adopt the TMAP program, which was called PennMAP, and it looked like the rest of the country would also fall in line because President Bush had put together a health commission to promote the initiative. According to the Bush commissioners, children of all ages, including preschoolers, needed screening. As stated in their report, testing of many millions of adolescents was necessary because "each year, young children are expelled from preschools and childcare facilities for severely disruptive behaviors and emotional disorders."[46] Antipsychotics were apparently the answer.

Frustrated that his TMAP findings had been dismissed by his superiors, Jones packed two file boxes of evidence of pharmaceutical companies' bribery and filed a retaliation lawsuit against his former employers and, in 2006, joined the Texas attorney general to file a state False Claims Act case. As he later told a jury, he felt that patients who were automatically switched to drugs such as Risperdal were "being betrayed by the people who were supposed to [be] taking care of them."[47]

One would naturally think that once such revelations as TMAP became public information that corporate sponsorships of this kind would be held to greater scrutiny. I'm sorry to say that this is not the case. In fact, popular so-called "independent" health websites, such as WebMD, are doing exactly what TMAP first pioneered, only they continue to get away with it.

As first reported by CBS with a follow-up by the *Washington Post*, no matter which of the 10 answers a web user chose on WebMD's online test for depression, the result came out the same: "You may be at risk for major depression." The suggested remedy, of course, was to discuss your options (medication) with a physician.[48]

More troublesome still is what visitors aren't told about these websites and others owned by WebMD, including Drugs.com, MedicineNet, RxList, and theHeart.org.[49] The WebMD depression test was sponsored by Eli Lilly, the maker of anti-depression drug Cymbalta. Further, WebMD's investors at one time included chemical giant DuPont and Rupert Murdoch's News Corp.

What completes these conflicts of interest and blurs the line between ads and independent content is the company's partnership with the FDA.[50]

CHAPTER 13: THE FDA: FEDERAL DRUG ACCOMPLICE

I didn't know Dorothy Wilson, or "Dot," as she liked to be called, when she was healthy. She reached out to me only after she fell gravely ill. A manager for the Unisys Corporation, a computer technology company in Blue Bell, Pa., she had been an altogether healthy woman in May of 1988. At age forty-three, she walked or jogged two miles each day, worked out, swam regularly at a health club, enjoyed cooking, reading, and movies, and spent much of her free time caring for her aging mother. Her only complaint was insomnia, a result of having to travel for her work. She simply couldn't sleep comfortably in hotel room beds. This was why she visited her physician. She wanted something to help her sleep. An extremely health-conscious woman, she wanted a medication that was non-addictive, and had no potentially dangerous side effects.

Her physician recommended non-prescription L-tryptophan, a naturally-occurring amino acid found in turkey and milk. A designated "natural product," which had been on store shelves for more than a decade, the FDA had a checkered history of regulating it and other amino acids used as dietary supplements.

In the late 1970s, as evidence began to mount of potentially harmful effects, the agency launched a crackdown and seized several shipments. But manufacturers sued, and the FDA soon backed off.

Wilson, like the general public, was unaware of this conflict between regulators and the dietary supplement industry, which had swirled in the background for years but had gotten no national exposure. For her, L-tryptophan at first seemed to work just fine.

So well, in fact, that she stopped taking it after three months. Around the same time, however, in August 1988, she noticed something unusual. After her regular lunch break walks, she experienced extreme weariness in her legs. She initially dismissed it as work-related fatigue or over-exertion, but the weariness didn't go away even after she cut back on her exercise and spent a long weekend relaxing in bed.

She said she also began to feel "strange" all over. She had dull, aching, intermittent pains. Sensing something wasn't right, she returned to her physician and underwent a battery of tests, which revealed nothing.

But her pain increased with each new week. That December, she took a short-term disability leave to undergo more comprehensive blood work tests at a hospital. The results showed a curious combination of symptoms. She had elevated liver enzymes, a high white blood cell count, and an extremely high count of something called eosinophils, commonly related to an allergic reaction or parasitosis. Yet, the specialists didn't have any answers and the pains continued, growing worse.

Back in the hospital, she underwent another battery of tests. Physicians now discovered extensive nerve damage throughout her body and a suspicious breast mass, which turned out to be cancer. She had a mastectomy, her symptoms stabilized, and for a time the strange aches and pains gradually diminished. Relieved, she went back to work and tried to resume her previous health regimen.

But she wasn't sleeping, so she resumed taking L-tryptophan.

Then, like a recurring nightmare, the strange symptoms returned, only now they were worse. In addition to the pins-and-needles-like aches and pains, she developed an itchy rash, and suffered fevers and night sweats.

The skin all over her body hardened and tightened.

After a month back on the L-tryptophan, this once-active career woman was unable to stand up from a chair and was confined to bed. She couldn't cough or sneeze without shooting pains and a burning sensation.

By November of 1989, virtually the only thing she could do by herself was to sit in bed and watch television. While watching TV one evening, she saw a CNN news report on a puzzling new disease with symptoms identical to her own. Something called eosinophilia-myalgia syndrome (EMS) was injuring people across the country. A few had died. All were in extreme pain. The one thing that connected all the EMS sufferers was L-tryptophan, most specifically L-tryptophan produced by manufacturer Showa Denko, a major Japanese petrochemical maker.

She decided then that she needed a lawyer.

When I met Dot, despite her myriad health problems, she jutted out her chin and flashed me a sassy smile. Her positive outlook, the kindness she exhibited to her caregivers, and her appreciation of life, despite the curve balls, were an inspiration. I wanted to help her and would do everything within my power to do so.

So, I quickly filed suit on her behalf. I may not have been the first attorney to go up against Showa Denko, but I was near the head of an increasingly long line. The truth of what happened emerged in August 1990. Then, Michael Osterholm, an investigator at the Minnesota Department of Health and future director of the Center for Infectious Disease Research at the University of Minnesota, reported that the implicated L-tryptophan had been produced by a bacteria that was genetically engineered in Showa Denko laboratories to produce higher-yield L-tryptophan.

But, by the time the FDA had moved to protect U.S. consumers from the tainted batches, more than 1,500 persons had become ill, like Dot Wilson, with EMS. In the end, congressional investigators laid blame for the outbreak squarely at the feet of the FDA, which had failed to respond to a growing body of evidence in the late 1980s that L-tryptophan and other amino acid-based, over-the-counter dietary supplements, while potentially useful as sleep aids, had been linked with a variety of deleterious health effects as well and thus were deserving of far more scrutiny than they were getting.

Among other things, congressional investigators said the FDA failed to respond when some manufacturers made false and illegal medicinal claims about their products.

This is how Rep. Patsy Mink, then chair of the House Human Resources and Intergovernmental Relations subcommittee, put it following a months' long probe by her panel of the L-tryptophan disaster:

> "Throughout the 1980s, the FDA permitted all amino acids to be marketed illegally as dietary supplements. Many of these products made illegal drug claims that were also ignored by the agency. What is perhaps most alarming, in my opinion, is the fact that all of the amino acids on the market today flaunt federal law and this sends (the worst) kind of signal... We fail to understand how FDA can allow the supplement industry to flaunt Federal law."

Were the FDA's failures regarding dietary supplements an isolated example of bureaucratic ineptitude and misfeasance, the public might have reason for some confidence.

But the FDA's deeply flawed record dates back decades and continues to this day, much to the detriment of the public it is supposed to protect. Time and again, the agency has approved drugs that cause harm to patients, and then turned away as evidence of harmful effects mounted, and more and more patients were harmed.

It is frightening how often this question has been asked and how little follow-through there has been:

"Why didn't the FDA require a warning of possible side effects?"

The list of harmful prescription medications and other products that were either approved for public consumption or escaped FDA regulation until it was too late, includes not only L-tryptophan, but also DES, Vioxx, various breast implant products, Risperdal, Fen-Phen, Seroquel, various vaginal mesh products and many others. After decades litigating on behalf of injured patients, poring through FDA filings and pharmaceutical company records, and witnessing first-hand the harm to unsuspecting consumers like Dot Wilson, I can only conclude the FDA has repeatedly violated the public trust and failed in its most basic mission.

How this happened is a classic tale of a regulated industry capturing control of the agency that supposedly is overseeing it. Through user fees authorized by Congress, big pharma has poured hundreds of millions of dollars into the FDA to support its operations. Its executives and scientific thought leaders shuttle back and forth through a revolving door between senior industry positions and leadership roles at the FDA. The result is an agency that sees itself more as a service provider to the industry than a tough-minded regulator whose highest purpose is the protection of public health. Against this backdrop, it is only natural that the industry point of view prevails, and profit takes precedence over public safety.

Once in a while, a courageous FDA whistleblower will step forward to alert the public to exactly what is going on. But these isolated events only serve to underscore the degree to which the FDA is in the thrall of drug makers.

One particularly explosive disclosure occurred in 2004 when Dr. David Graham, an associate director for science and medicine in the FDA's office of drug safety, revealed the results of research showing that Vioxx, an anti-inflammatory Cox-2 inhibitor marketed by Merck & Co., had been associated with as much as a four-fold increase in heart attacks. Graham estimated the drug was responsible for as many as 139,000 excess heart attacks annually, up to 40 percent of them fatal.

Under pressure, Merck eventually withdrew the medication from the market, but when Graham first tried to raise the alarm within the FDA he came under withering internal criticism.

In at least one instance, he was pressured by his superiors to change the conclusions of a study raising the alarm about Vioxx. He was told that if he refused, he would be barred from delivering a talk on the study at an upcoming scientific conference.

One FDA official went so far as to label Graham's findings a "scientific rumor."

Yet, even as Graham was compiling information showing that Vioxx posed a risk, the FDA approved its use for children with rheumatoid arthritis.

The problem, Graham said, is regulators become professionally and emotionally invested in the drugs they approve. As a consequence, they're highly resistant to information showing harmful side effects. It's tough, in other words, to admit making a mistake.

Graham said his experience with Vioxx was typical of how the FDA's Center for Drug Evaluation and Research, which is the gatekeeper for new medications and is responsible for establishing their safety before they are brought to market, responded to serious drug safety issues. The center and the FDA's Office of New Drugs were "extremely resistant" to full and open disclosure of safety information, especially when an existing regulatory position was called into question.

"In these situations, the new drug reviewing division that approved the drug in the first place and that regards it as its own child, typically proves to be the single greatest obstacle to effectively dealing with serious drug safety issues," Graham said in Senate testimony.

Graham was not alone in his criticism. For years, CDER and its director, Janet Woodcock, have been a lightning-rod for many other FDA critics.

In 2005, despite ongoing questions regarding the FDA's oversight of the drug industry and its ability to react to post marketing reports of dangerous drug reactions, Woodcock testified before Congress that new legislation wasn't necessary to give the agency more authority to require additional clinical trials or order label changes for drugs when safety questions arise after approval.

Her testimony directly contradicted that of her colleague Sandra Kweder, then deputy director of the Office of New Drugs at the FDA.

In testimony only 48 hours before Woodcock's appearance, Kweder said the FDA needed clear authority to assess risk and change labeling, and that patients needed and deserved information in "understandable language." Kweder told the committee that at the time the FDA could only persuade, not force, drug companies to change labels or withdraw a drug from the market. Label changes, she said, required exhaustive negotiations with the companies, which led to long delays in remedial action. Meantime, consumers were harmed. To put this in perspective, both women were appearing on Capitol Hill around the time I received my first frantic call about Risperdal.

During her testimony in 2005 and in appearances since then, Woodcock has touted the agency's ability to get updated drug information on risks as they're discovered out to consumers quickly. But a year later, Woodcock seemed to contradict herself. When GlaxoSmithKline provided the results of its internal analyses of the diabetes drug Avandia to the FDA, showing that it raised the risk of heart attacks by 31 percent, the agency didn't immediately release those studies to the public because regulators "didn't necessarily agree with some of the methodology used," Woodcock said, according to court documents. It was an odd position for the FDA to take. Here was a company disclosing information to the FDA that could conceivably impede sales of its own product. If anything, the economic incentives would seem to weigh against Glaxo coming forward with that information unless the company was seriously concerned.

But it wasn't until April of 2006 that the FDA asked that the drug's label be updated with new data in the warnings section.

On the FDA's role in the drug development process, Woodcock has likened the agency's oversight to that of a building inspector. "Someone else builds the building according to code," Woodcock said. The FDA writes the code, and then comes in at the end and inspects the results to make sure they're up to code, she said.

In my view, the problem is the code is flawed from the start and the inspectors are in cahoots with the builder. One reason is the revolving door between the FDA and the pharmaceutical industry. Research published in September 2016 by the BMJ, previously known as the British Medical Journal, found that more than a quarter of FDA employees who approved cancer and hematology drugs between 2001 and 2010 left the agency to work for pharmaceutical companies.[51] At the same time, prominent politicians who draft and vote on legislation impacting how government regulates the industry and thus the very core of its business join powerful industry groups once they retire from Congress. Such was the case with former Louisiana Congressman Billy Tauzin, a Republican, who took over as head of the Pharmaceutical Research and Manufacturers of America, at an annual salary of $11 million, after chairing the powerful House Energy and

Commerce Committee.[52]

Energy and Commerce had oversight responsibility for, among other industries, the pharmaceutical industry. His fellow Republican, former congressman James Greenwood, who chaired the House Subcommittee on Oversight and Investigations, went on to head up the Biotechnology Innovation Organization in 2005, the Washington based trade group of the biotech industry, after he stepped down from his House seat in 2005.

Congress enacted the Food, Drug and Cosmetic Act in 1938, greatly expanding the powers of the FDA in response to the deaths of scores of children killed by sulfanilamide, a hideous pseudo medicine that was formulated using anti-freeze. Under the act, manufacturers were required to perform toxicity testing and to supply safety information to the FDA prior to a drug's approval.

Then in 1962, in response to the thalidomide disaster in Europe, which caused birth defects in as many as 10,000 children born to women who had been given the drug as a treatment for morning sickness, Congress amended the law. The Kefauver-Harris amendments revolutionized drug development by calling for increased scrutiny of toxicity and adding a requirement that companies prove a drug's efficacy before it's marketed.[53] To fully understand the conflicting loyalties that now plague the FDA, one has to go back to the unholy union created between the agency and the pharmaceutical industry back in 1992. That year, Congress passed the Prescription Drug User Fee Act, which was meant to help the agency alleviate staffing issues that resulted in a slow drug approval process. PDUFA, as it is known, authorized the FDA to collect industry user fees to hire additional staff and upgrade its internal systems.

But that meant the FDA would be funded to a large extent by the very industry that it is supposed to monitor. The conflict is hard to ignore.

And the sums are enormous.

User fee collections have grown from roughly $71 million in 1995 to $884 million in 2016. One report released in 2016 puts total collection at almost $8 billion since the passage of the Act. The Congressional Budget Office says the FDA could collect an additional

$8 billion in fees for drugs between 2018 and 2022.[54]

The FDA's myriad problems are enough to fill a book of its own and maybe one day I'll write it. However, until then, I can't close this chapter without mentioning one other significant misstep that reflects the agency's failure to improve its procedures for the benefit of public health. In 2015, the Journal of the American Medical Association published the results of its review of 57 clinical trials in which researchers had falsified data or otherwise violated FDA protocols. Results of those trials were published in 78 peer-reviewed articles, but the findings of procedural violations were mentioned in only three publications. Thus, key information about the reliability of those studies was not made available to physicians and others in the medical community who may have been making decisions on how to treat patients based on study information that was incomplete at best and possibly fraudulent at worst.

STEPHEN A. SHELLER

CHAPTER 14: CULPABILITY IN THE COURTS

Sometimes it seems my clients are locked in a kind of asymmetrical warfare where corporate America has the equivalent of a powerful fleet of F-15 fighter jets while plaintiffs are equipped with infantry rifles pointlessly plinking away at the heavy forces arrayed against them.

While rogue pharmaceutical companies have inflicted enormous harm on their customers, the odds for obtaining justice keep getting longer.

How did we get here?

For answers, it's useful to take a close look at how the civil justice system in Philadelphia has evolved. The arc of changes that have taken place there pretty much mirror what has happened elsewhere in the U.S. In the late 1970s, as plaintiffs' personal injury litigation exploded across the country, the Philadelphia court system gained a reputation for efficient case management and swift results for defendants and injured parties alike.

Judicial leaders created a complex litigation center where technically challenging cases would be overseen by judges steeped in the law and science of subject areas from asbestos poisoning to malfunctioning medical devices like the ghoulish vaginal mesh treatments that maimed tens of thousands of women and harmful prescription drugs, among many, many other personal injury disputes.

The center's reputation for skillfully adjudicating legal disputes over harmful products involving injury claims of hundreds of millions, if not billions, of dollars served to make it a model for other state level court systems nationwide.

But where the civil justice system once offered at least the prospect of justice, it now regularly frustrates my clients' quest to be compensated for the injuries and harm they have suffered.

The truth of the matter is that in ways large and small the courts are now failing citizens by throwing up roadblocks to a just resolution of their cases, often at the behest of big corporations that are looking to limit their losses.

The seeds of this terrible reversal, ironically, were contained in our early successes. As my practice grew over the years, we became more and more effective in holding corporate wrongdoers to account. In the tobacco litigation, in the DES lawsuits and in our litigation against the makers of defective breast implants and atypical antipsychotics such as Seroquel, we won huge awards against drug companies and medical device makers, or prepared cases that were so strong companies had no choice but to settle, often on terms that were highly advantageous to my clients.

So, it was to be expected then that corporate America eventually would counter attack. And when the assault came, it was launched on multiple fronts. Business groups funded something called the Institute for Legal Reform that sought to implement restrictions in state capitols nationwide on the rights of individuals to sue.

Corporate interests helped finance the judicial campaigns of judges that were openly hostile to the cause of plaintiffs. And well financed defense firms mounted multiple strategies to frustrate plaintiffs seeking access to the courts to redress grievances.

One of the most effective strategies was a business and physician funded campaign to identify what they called America's top "Judicial Hellholes," places where plaintiffs' lawyers supposedly ran rampant and judges and juries quashed the rights of corporate defendants. The campaign had the desired effect. Court jurisdictions unlucky enough to be placed on the list were stigmatized and often local court administrators bent over backwards to take steps to insure their jurisdictions were taken off the list.

Philadelphia was no exception. When it was named a top judicial hellhole in 2011 and 2012, court administrators there sought to impose a series of restrictions aimed at reducing the backlog of asbestos and prescription drug lawsuits, most notably by making it more difficult for out of town lawyers to litigate personal injury cases in the city. For a time, out of town depositions were banned and punitive damages were put on hold. The changes had their desired effect because a short time later, Philadelphia's designation as the nation's number one judicial hellhole —deeply mortifying to the city's court administrators and the bar generally—was removed; although the city has remained on the list as a problematic jurisdiction for defense lawyers.

But not without consequences. Campaigns like the judicial hellhole initiative have tilted the playing field unfairly in the direction of well-funded corporations and against plaintiffs.

If there is one corporate lawyer responsible for the mostly successful counterattack by American business against plaintiffs' class actions, it probably is Alan Kaplinsky.

Kaplinsky, a senior partner at the Philadelphia based law firm of Ballard Spahr, was an obscure lawyer for banks and credit card companies in the mid-1990s, when he hit upon a novel idea. Why not require cardholders to take their claims to an arbitrator instead of going to court, while also waiving the right to file a class-action lawsuit?

Kaplinsky was obscure no more. His brainstorm was applauded by financial services companies, which quickly adopted the practice for credit card agreements and many other consumer transactions all across the nation. It also spawned outrage among plaintiffs' lawyers, and efforts on Capitol Hill and in the Obama administration to sharply restrict the use of arbitration. One result is the Consumer Financial Protection Bureau, authorized by Congress in response to the 2008 credit crunch. It eventually adopted regulations barring financial firms from requiring customers to waive the right to file a class action lawsuit.

It's easy to see why corporate America would want such a restriction. With the ban against consumers filing class actions against credit card companies and other financial services providers, consumers were effectively denied the ability to band together to fight unfair treatment. Individual complaints did not offer the scale of lawsuits representing tens of thousands of plaintiffs and couldn't support the high underlying cost of such litigation, so in the end very few were filed.

In its analysis of the impact of the waiver on the rights to credit card customers and others to sue their financial services companies, the CFPB found that while millions of consumers are covered by class-action waivers and arbitration requirements, only a few hundred sought to arbitrate complaints during the period studied, from 2010 to 2012.

"The use of class-action waivers has evolved to the point where it effectively functions as a kind of legal lockout," said former bureau director Richard Cordray, who has since been replaced by Mick Mulvaney, President Trump's former director of the Office of Management and Budget. "Companies simply insert these clauses into their contracts for consumer financial products or services and literally with the stroke of a pen are able to block any group of consumers from filing...class actions."

So, it's not just the FDA that has created the crisis in pharmaceutical industry oversight, nor just politicians who are to blame for permitting an industry to place profit above patient safety. The courts have just as much on the line with oftentimes bizarre rulings that help to keep drug maker wrongdoing under wraps. In the case of J&J and its subsidiary Janssen, crucial information about Risperdal's risks stayed hidden for 13 years despite my many attempts to make it public.

Janssen took away the public's choice when it came to this drug. But it had a lot of help from a judicial system that at times can seem stubbornly blind to the glaring truth. Rather than serve as the arbiters of justice, the courts have unintentionally aided and abetted Janssen's misconduct with rulings that make it impossible for cases to move ahead or for the truth to emerge. They took away the right of parents to make the best decisions for their children and they took away the rights of doctors to make the best choices for their pediatric patients. They also took away the rights of the children to safe and effective drugs for their ailments. Claims relating to the association between Risperdal and gynecomastia are pending in courts all over this country. While this litigation plays out, Risperdal and its generic version risperidone remain on the market. For that we have a court system to blame that is too attentive to corporate interests and too little concerned with what can only be described as an ongoing public health catastrophe.

The protective order in the Risperdal cases remains in full effect and governs the use of confidential documents and information. It can only be amended or superseded by court order. The onerous restrictions remain even after the conclusion of the Risperdal litigation.

In addition to shutting me down at every turn in my quest to make Risperdal documents public, the courts have also restricted the amount of damages we can seek and threatened to dismiss a slew of cases on grounds that they were filed too late, using legal standards that recall all too precisely the bureaucratic tangles so devastatingly portrayed by author Joseph Heller in the novel Catch-22.

When a pharmaceutical company produces a drug, it enters into an agreement of trust with the medical community and the public. Regulatory authorities trust the company has abided and will abide by rules requiring them to study and accurately report on the adverse effects of their products.

Healthcare providers expect the same and trust that the labels and indications for drug products they give their patients are in accordance with all the available information. Patients also trust their doctor has been warned of the risks of a drug and can weigh them against the benefits with confidence in that decision. From at least as early as 2002, Janssen has betrayed that trust. The company has misled the public into thinking its product is safer and was allowed by the courts to hide this betrayal behind a protective order.

In hopes of keeping its misdeeds out of the public eye, Janssen made blanket assertions in the Risperdal litigation that documents requested by plaintiffs contained "proprietary, confidential or private information" yet couldn't point to any specific material that should be protected. Neither could the company support its requests with affidavits from any of its corporate officers stating that the information requests would reveal company trade secrets that would result in competitive injury.

Like the claims of Risperdal's safety, these assertions could not withstand scrutiny.

Yet the courts have been inexplicably sympathetic to Johnson & Johnson's arguments, often issuing rulings that severely restrict what we can make public, what we can question company executives about and even how we use information gathered pre-trial as evidence during a case.

For Janssen officials, patient injuries, a potential criminal investigation and litigation are a relatively small cost of doing business. To this day, the J&J subsidiary still hasn't been forthright with healthcare providers nor the public, betraying the trust of the medical community and robbing patients of the right to make informed decisions about their health. The company continues to keep secret information that would help regulators ensure the proper warnings on labels.

I'm not opposed to taking medicine and this book isn't meant to be an indictment of the value of medicine in improving our lives. However, drug manufacturers should be obligated to ensure that people who decide to take their drug, or give it to their children, do so with knowledge of all the risks.

Since 2009, I've been fighting the courts to make documents detailing the dangers of Risperdal public. In all, five judges and an appeals court turned down more than five requests to undo a blanket confidentiality order protecting Janssen's documents that would show the dangers of Risperdal. This doesn't include my petition to another four judges and a second appeals court seeking the drug's removal from the market based on the erroneous reports J&J submitted to win FDA approval.

Let me put this in context for you: since the start of our litigation over Risperdal, Janssen produced about 2.6 million documents. This massive document dump, a strategy sometimes used by defendants to overwhelm the typically smaller plaintiff's staff, included more than 20 million pages of information. Janssen audaciously claimed that 96 percent of what they gave us should be marked confidential.

The tremendous public interest in the case, and the data and materials being hidden by Janssen, outweigh the company's claims to secrecy, I wrote to a New Jersey judge at the time. If the documents are truly "observations regarding efficacy, risks and benefits and side effects," then they cannot be proprietary and should instead be viewed as safety documents that require disclosure for the well-being of the public.

Janssen argued there was "no legitimate purpose" to be served by declassifying the documents. However, years later the company would reveal its true fear, writing that I had expressed the intent and desire to provide certain documents to the press and petition the FDA to revoke various approvals for Risperdal use in children and adolescents.

We would eventually find out in the Pledger case, more than six years after our initial request to the judge in New Jersey, just how much damning evidence the company hid.

I first requested a waiver from the confidentiality protections governing Janssen's documents in May 2009. At the time my office was representing about 30 boys and young men who had enlarged breast tissue from taking Risperdal. There was information we uncovered in Janssen documents and the testimony of certain company witnesses that we had a public health emergency on our hands. Buried in the mountains of information we got were details that put the pediatric rate of developing gynecomastia at 12.5 percent, far more than the 2.3 percent listed on the drug's current label. The reported rate, we found, was a combination of short and long-term usage data even though all approved pediatric prescriptions were for chronic, long-term use.

Documents produced by Janssen pointed not only to a much higher rate, but they also suggested that children were susceptible to gynecomastia after just eight months of use. In another shocking revelation, we found that a former Janssen child and adolescent marketing director, who authored one of the company's white papers on prolactin, didn't even know the definition of gynecomastia. If this person who worked at the company for five years had no idea what gynecomastia was, how then could a parent be expected to know?

It was evident to us that we had uncovered a public health emergency that put boys at a heightened risk of gynecomastia if they took the drug for a prolonged period. We begged the New Jersey judge and a special panel of former judges she appointed to hear our request to allow us to make the information public. The intentional concealment of the true rates of gynecomastia trumped, in my view, Janssen's confidentiality concerns.

New Jersey law governing the confidentiality of documents favors public access, especially when it comes to public health. Our argument was that the public's need to know all the risks and benefits of Risperdal exceeded any possible interest of the company in privacy.

Janssen argued exactly the opposite, that the doctors and the public only needed to know what was in the FDA-approved label. The company went even further, accusing us of trying to frighten parents so they would discontinue their child's use of the medicine. What's more, the company even claimed that gynecomastia was a common and reversible clinical condition that required no medical treatment or intervention. That simply wasn't true!

The truth was that Janssen had hidden serious and harmful information about Risperdal's link to gynecomastia for the company's own gain.

In fact, sales of Risperdal increased from $892 million to $2 billion per year between 1999 and 2005. By 2009, annual sales topped $4.7 billion. By then the drug was approved to treat schizophrenia and bipolar disorder in children as young as 13 and it was being marketed by various means to its younger clientele.

We convinced the panel of former judges in 2009 to send our request back to the trial judge with their recommendation that the information we sought be made public for the sole purpose of petitioning the FDA for a label change. I thought we had finally scored a victory but Judge Jessica Mayer, who had recently joined the bench after a career with a prominent New Jersey defense firm, shattered those hopes on Oct. 30, 2009, when she ruled that the information would be kept under wraps.

Her reasoning: excessive publicity would taint the jury selection process against the company.

At the same time, the judge lamented that this type of litigation, mass tort as it's known, would be more expensive and burdensome without blanket umbrella protective orders. Expensive and burdensome for whom? Corporate defendants, presumably. But does that justify keeping the public in the dark about potentially harmful drugs? So we took our appeal to a higher court. It rejected our argument without explanation. I tried twice more in Pennsylvania to make documents public and both times was rejected by two separate judges, Judge Sandra Moss in 2011 and Judge Arnold New in 2014, this during the time that the Philadelphia civil justice system had come under assault by the U.S. Chamber of Commerce. It wasn't until 2015 during Austin Pledger's trial that the public would learn of Janssen's misdeeds and that the company did in fact withhold information from the FDA. Former FDA Commissioner David Kessler, serving as an expert witness for our side, testified about two studies conducted in 2002 which showed that children who had taken Risperdal for as long as two years, developed gynecomastia at a rate of 12.5 percent: much higher than Janssen's reported 2.3 percent.

Janssen's non-disclosure wasn't accidental, Kessler said. In fact, the company sought to bury the evidence by deleting a table that showed the unfavorable data resulting in the higher rate and instead pooling children tested across all Risperdal studies into one report, so a smaller incidence rate could be shown. This was the very conduct we warned the New Jersey court about years earlier, the very court that refused to take our concerns seriously.

Austin was prescribed Risperdal when he was eight years old and took the drug for five years beginning in the summer of 2002. He had been on the drug for eight weeks by the time the data showing the 12.5 percent rate began circulating through Janssen's offices. Janssen officials knew at the time that those children who had abnormal prolactin levels between weeks eight and 12 had a significant statistical chance of developing gynecomastia in the future if they were kept on Risperdal. Still, the company failed to sound alarm bells, failed to warn doctors and never authorized its sales reps to give warnings when they gave out drug samples. In February 2015, the jury in the Pledger case caught the company in its lie and decided on a $2.5 million compensatory judgment. Think of how much more it would have been, and how much more just the result would have been, if punitive damages had not been prohibited by Judge New. An appeal of New's decision would eventually work out in our favor, but more on that later. It was apparent that Janssen hid damaging information about Risperdal's risks for 13 years and the concealment had finally caught up with the company.

A year after the Pledger verdict, another jury was asked to consider whether Janssen intentionally falsified, destroyed or concealed records pertaining to material evidence in the case. The response was a resounding yes with jurors finding Janssen liable for $70 million in damages to Andrew Yount, a teenager from Tennessee who developed gynecomastia at age five.

But there were setbacks. In 2014, New overturned a previous ruling by deciding that punitive damages—those intended to punish a defendant for negligence or out and out misconduct—would not be allowed in Risperdal personal injury cases. Under New's reasoning, the company wasn't subject to punitive damages because it is headquartered in New Jersey, where punitive damages are banned under state product liability laws. This is no doubt why Janssen, J&J, and so many other pharmaceutical companies are headquartered there.

Never mind that Risperdal injuries, such as those experienced by Austin Pledger, occurred throughout the United States and that Janssen's previous position was that punitive damages should be based on the law of the state where the drug was marketed, prescribed, and ingested. Also, never mind that Janssen committed breaches of FDA rules by withholding from the FDA clinical trial results linking Risperdal to gynecomastia and that its sales reps were flogging its unapproved-by-the-FDA off-label "benefits" to physicians in violation of federal law. Judge New declared such issues would have no impact on New Jersey's product liability statutes.

In another instance of a court siding with a drug manufacturer against an injured patient, a Pennsylvania judge ruled that a 17-year-old, who was prescribed the drug for anger issues, should have known by June 30, 2009 that his development of breasts more than a decade earlier was linked to his use of the drug. That defies logic, considering that in 2009, the company was in the midst of its scheme to hide damaging risk information. That was also the year I first requested that the information we found be made public. Remember, it was the courts that rejected my request. The information I sought wouldn't be revealed until the Pledger trial in 2015, so how could a 17-year-old have known before then that his large, female-like breasts were a result of taking Risperdal? How was he to know in any of the years up until 2009 that Risperdal caused his injuries and his mental anguish if the company hid the information behind bogus marketing propaganda?

To underscore this point, just take a look at the label. While it does warn that Risperdal causes weight gain, it doesn't alert users that extra weight could, and does, mask detection of gynecomastia, which is the growth of female breast tissue. What this means is that the parents of children on Risperdal could simply assume they're gaining weight and would be unaware that they're in fact developing female breasts. In addition, the company's major defense is a Catch-22.

On the one hand, J&J argues that the weight gain is simply extra fat and not gynecomastia. On the other hand, when children and their parents and the courts allege that the statute of limitations cannot begin to run until such time they knew they had developed breast tissue, the company argues they should have known they were developing breasts and that it wasn't simply extra weight. By failing to find out whether they were developing breast tissue, within two years of the time they gained weight, the statute of limitations would have expired, the company argued.

Further, in a disheartening upset that has sadly become the new trend in the conservative higher courts, corporation-friendly state supreme court justices in Louisiana and Arkansas have now reversed lower court verdicts against J&J. How the decision makers justified the reversals differs, but in Arkansas, the court interpreted the Arkansas Medicaid Fraud False Claims Act and the Arkansas Deceptive Trade Practices Act (MFFCA) to say that only healthcare facilities can be liable in their state for wrongdoing under the act and as J&J is not a healthcare facility it shouldn't be held accountable.

Such an interpretation of the law may be justified, but what of the injured plaintiffs? Does J&J bear no responsibility?

CHAPTER 15: HOLDING PHARMA EXECS TO ACCOUNT

When the energy trading firm Enron filed for bankruptcy in December 2001 amid allegations of offshore accounts and billions in missing funds, Republicans in Washington began to panic.

Enron's collapse not only wiped out the savings of tens of thousands of retirees, it also unleashed a financial market collapse that rippled powerfully through the economy, bringing job losses and widespread financial hardship.

Faced with a potential election backlash and the loss of the Republican House majority, the administration of President George W. Bush, normally closely allied with big business, set up a corporate fraud task force at the Justice Department to crack down on corporate abuse.

There was a transparently self-serving aspect to this. Bush had been the subject of sustained attacks by Democrats during the 2000 presidential campaign and at the advent of his administration alleging that he was too close to corporate interests. Ken Lay, the disgraced former president and CEO of Enron, was a major Republican supporter and was so well known in the Bush camp that the former president bestowed a coveted nickname on him, "Kenny Boy."

Lest any evidence was needed of Bush's precarious political standing, his razor thin – and disputed – election victory just months earlier all too clearly showed that his support was fragile.

With their political survival on the line, Republicans set about to signal to the public that they would crack down on corporate abuses.

And crack down they did. Within a few years, the Justice Department's corporate fraud task force, which included among others

Christopher Wray, now the FBI director, had racked up scores of convictions. Notably, Enron executives Jeffrey Skilling and Andy Fastow went to jail, as did Bernie Ebbers, the former president and CEO of then telecommunications giant WorldCom.

Contrast that all-out attack on corporate misfeasance – instigated as it was by Republican fears that they would soon be thrown out of office by furious voters – with Justice Department practice today. Where the Justice Department had once been tough on corporate crime, federal prosecutors in recent years, under both Republican and Democratic administrations, have shown themselves to be highly reluctant to criminally charge corporate executives.

Instead, they've opted for settlements in which companies admit to some level of misconduct and pay what seems to be an enormous fine. But individual executives who may have orchestrated the misdeeds get off scot free. Now, corporations caught in the government's cross hairs typically sign a deferred prosecution agreement imposing fines and requiring the company to admit to and correct offending behavior. Typically, no individual executive is punished nor are any even named in these settlements.

There is no more telling example of this retreat by the government in the face of rampant corporate excess than the fallout, or lack of it, from the Risperdal litigation. Despite the scandal of corporate fraud and malfeasance that was exposed through discovery in our litigation and the government's criminal probe, Johnson & Johnson paid little for the harm that it inflicted on the public.

No J&J or Janssen executives, or even low-ranking sales reps, went to jail or were charged with a crime. Like its competitors at Eli Lilly, AstraZeneca, and Pfizer, J&J cut a deal: in return for immunity from felony prosecution in 2013, the company paid a fine and pleaded guilty to a single misdemeanor charge. And this, shamefully, for off-label marketing to the elderly, not children. The marketing of Risperdal to the elderly, given studies showing a link between heart attacks and strokes among elderly users, is disturbing enough. But the harm to children, tens of thousands of whom likely suffered gynecomastia as a result of taking the drug, is no less appalling.

Yet it was a particularly insidious aspect of this settlement that

J&J was permitted by the Justice Department to escape a guilty plea for marketing to children, despite substantial evidence that they were targeted by Janssen sales reps. The benefits to J&J were enormous. The bulk of the litigation against the company for improperly marketing Risperdal comprises plaintiffs who had taken the drug as children. Although elderly victims had suffered harm, proving that their heart attacks and strokes resulted from taking Risperdal and not the effects of aging would have been a high hurdle. But had J&J pleaded guilty to illegally marketing to children, its defenses against those lawsuits would have been substantially undermined. That the company never had to plead to that charge and that the $2.2 billion penalty amounted to only a quarter's worth of the company's annual profit, meant that the entire government case against J&J amounted to little more than a bump in the road.

In fact, J&J's stock price barely budged following disclosure of the settlement.

There are likely multiple reasons for the Justice Department backing off its once tough approach to corporate crime. While the Bush administration sought to inoculate itself with aggressive prosecutions against political attacks from the Enron collapse, those same criminal investigations also generated a backlash. And the reaction was particularly fierce with the indictment and conviction of Enron's auditor, Arthur Andersen, then one of the so-called Big Five accounting firms. Andersen was accused of destroying thousands of documents under subpoena by the SEC, which at the time had launched a probe of Enron's collapsing finances.

The evidence indicated that a relative handful of Andersen employees were responsible for the document destruction, yet the entire firm, with more than 90,000 employees, was criminally charged.

Andersen quickly collapsed—no auditing firm can legally perform its services while facing criminal charges – and that in turn caused indignation in some quarters of the legal profession, where the view prevailed that prosecutors had overreached. By bringing a criminal case against the entire firm, rather than a handful of employees, prosecutors had done more harm than good, or so the thinking went. The result was the destruction of a global consulting and accounting firm, putting tens of thousands out of work.

When the U.S. Supreme Court overturned the conviction a few years later citing flawed jury instructions by the trial judge, critics of the prosecution proclaimed their vindication. Ever since, the Justice Department has contented itself with hammering out settlements like the agreement with J&J over its illegal off-label marketing of Risperdal.

One other factor weighed into this relatively forgiving approach. Among the ranks of career prosecutors, it is a commonly accepted premise that white-collar crime prosecutions of senior executives of sprawling, multi-national corporations are complex and fraught with risk. Proving criminal intent against an executive who may be several levels removed from the illegal actions themselves poses difficult evidentiary hurdles.

The temptation to settle under those circumstances can be enormous. Why risk career and reputation with a failed criminal investigation when a case can be settled, with the Justice Department touting a big fine and promises by the errant corporation to mend its ways?

I believe this kind of prosecutorial timidity has made efforts of plaintiffs' lawyers like myself all the more critical to the goal of achieving justice.

The jury is still out on the impact our litigation may have on the careers of executives who made the marketing decisions involving Risperdal and other harmful drugs. I do, however, have reason to be modestly hopeful that our message has gotten through and that the public has come to understand the egregiously self-serving and harmful behavior of some pharmaceutical executives. The list of missteps is hardly limited to Risperdal. It also includes unprecedented product recalls of such J&J staples as Motrin, Rolaids, Tylenol, and Mylanta, and its reformulation of J&J's No More Tears baby shampoo and one hundred other baby products after they were discovered to contain potentially harmful chemicals, among them formaldehyde.

And that is in addition to recalls and litigation over J&J's defective hip implants, injury-inducing vaginal mesh devices, ovarian cancer-causing baby powder, and tendon-snapping, neurologically-damaging Levaquin antibiotic.

Among those who have gotten the message are disaffected stockholders, some of whom at one point took matters into their own hands with a lawsuit against J&J board members and several executives, including Gorsky and Weldon. They claimed that J&J's corporate directors and executives failed to stop criminal wrongdoing and misrepresentation of its products.[55] Another suit brought by one stockholder alleged that Weldon, who reportedly earned a combined $175 million from 2006 until his retirement, was grossly overpaid given the "highly publicized compliance failures, recalls, and misconduct" at J&J.[56]

Yet while J&J's reputation suffered, its CEO's annual compensation kept going up. Though I am pleased that stockholders and others have finally woken up to what has been going on, one can only wonder what was going through board members' minds when Weldon, who was voted one of the worst CEOs of 2011 by the *New York Times*, was permitted to choose Gorsky—at one point the head of sales and marketing at Janssen while the company engaged in so many questionable activities—to take his place. Perhaps I'll get to find out one day if I get to cross-examine him on the witness stand.

But I'm not terribly optimistic. The courts have repeatedly shielded him from cross-examination in this case as well as in another civil action, that one having to do with Exelon, the Alzheimer's treatment patch produced by Novartis, where Gorsky also worked.

I reference the Exelon case because, in my view, it reveals a similar pattern of behavior suggesting that executives knew exactly what their marketing departments were up to.

Gorsky, who had his start at Janssen as a sales rep and went on to become vice president of marketing and sales, and then CEO, left for Novartis in 2004, just after he succeeded in making Risperdal the biggest-selling drug in the company's history.

In 2007, the FDA wrote Gorsky accusing Novartis of making misleading claims about Exelon's efficacy and superiority to other treatments, in violation of federal law. The FDA said the misrepresentations were "concerning from a public health perspective because they suggest that Exelon is safer and more effective than has been demonstrated and they encourage the use of Exelon in circumstances other than those for which the drug has been shown to be safe and effective."

And what of Dr. Biederman who, to my mind, is just as responsible as Weldon and Gorsky for disseminating misleading information about Risperdal?

The Massachusetts General Hospital and Harvard Medical School took a step in the right direction by disciplining him in 2011.[57] As a consequence, Biederman and three other physicians were banned from pharmaceutical industry–sponsored "outside" activities for one year. When the ban ended, they also had to obtain permission from the hospital and Harvard Medical School before engaging in any industry-sponsored or paid outside activities for two additional years. In addition, they were required to undergo certain, unspecified training and faced delays in promotions or advancements.[58]

These consequences seemed like a slap on the wrist and are not what I had hoped for nor anticipated.

Biederman hasn't, for example, been asked to return the more than $1.6 million he earned from pharmaceutical companies for consulting fees. Nor have any efforts been made to rescind the awards for excellence he has received from the American Psychiatric Association nor the American Academy of Child and Adolescent Psychiatry. He remains in the Children and Adults with Attention-Deficit/Hyperactivity Disorder (CHADD) Hall of Fame.

Over the years, as evidence of Risperdal's dangers to children mounted, the government's enforcement and regulatory actions faltered. My frustration only grew as the FDA failed to act, either by strengthening the label or removing the drug from the market altogether. I finally took matters into my own hands in 2012, by filing a citizen's petition with the FDA to revoke approval for Risperdal, Invega, and all related generics until and unless the long-term safety of the products could be demonstrated.

I requested that the FDA, in its role as gatekeeper, review confidential documents that I had obtained in our litigation against J&J establishing the danger of Risperdal. These documents were damning. They showed a strong correlation between Risperdal and gynecomastia in children, but I couldn't release them on my own. They were subject to confidentiality and protective orders during the course of the litigation.

In the alternative, we argued that the FDA could simply instruct the company to release me from those orders so that I would be able to submit the documents myself. I knew it was a longshot, but it was a risk I felt compelled to take.

To bolster my case, I prepared and submitted to FDA Commissioner Margaret Hamburg a dossier containing copies of the court-permissible documents that outline and support the claims I made and will continue to make in civil court. I further requested that the FDA obtain the court's permission to review the many documents in my possession that are still under seal. Unfortunately for all concerned (except perhaps for J&J), after nearly two years waiting for a review of my submissions, Janet Woodcock rejected my petition. Rather than demand a long-term clinical study of Risperdal, Invega, and all related generics or order a probe of the documents I cited in my filings, the FDA chose instead to rely on J&J's word that it had already submitted all relevant material, clinical trial tests, and research to the agency and there was no need for further investigation.

In plain words, the FDA wouldn't review the evidence. Nevermind that I was representing hundreds of children harmed by this drug and that the attorney general had just settled with J&J for $2.2 billion. Why, you might ask, would a company settle for such a monumental penalty if it had not engaged in questionable conduct? Wouldn't you imagine that our government's drug regulatory agency would be interested in what the attorney general found?

Instead, Woodcock rationalized that there was no evidence the drug was unsafe and asserted that its withdrawal from the market would "constitute a disservice to the public health."

What makes Woodcock's decision all the more troubling is that J&J itself admitted during the course of our litigation that it had failed to turn over to the FDA research results showing the dangers of Risperdal. In his 2015 deposition, Ivo Caers, a J&J biochemist who had worked for the company for 36 years, said Janssen never disclosed to the FDA studies showing the risk of developing gynecomastia after taking the drug was as high as 12.5 percent. The company claimed later that the research had only ancillary value and that it wasn't a finished research product, but it is arguably the case that J&J was legally obligated to turn over that information to the FDA.

Had the company done so, it would have made it more difficult for the FDA to look the other way.

Around the time of Caers' testimony, I hired the law firm of Duane Morris to file a lawsuit in federal court over the FDA's denial. The firm argued on my behalf that the agency's refusal to consider the information I offered infected its entire decision-making process.

While U.S. District Judge Legrome Davis was somewhat sympathetic to my dilemma, he nevertheless ruled that my strict confidentiality agreement with Janssen was to blame for the documents remaining hidden from public view, and not the FDA's denial of my petition. Mind you, the agreement was necessary to even access Janssen's documents in the first place.

Interestingly, the U.S. Attorney in Philadelphia, whom I had just helped by delivering a solid whistleblower to make its case against J&J, argued on behalf of the FDA that my claim of spending thousands on litigation expenses did not constitute a valid injury, the basis of the lawsuit.

On appeal, the U.S. Court of Appeals for the Third Circuit in Philadelphia sided with the FDA and the government in October 2016, ruling that I had no standing to sue on behalf of the children and that the thousands of dollars I had already spent in my quest to save the lives of those children was the result of actions taken by me and Janssen, not the FDA.

So, I could claim no harm, at least a harm recognized by the Third Circuit. And even if the FDA had granted my petition revoking the drug's indication for children pending more robust long-term studies, the court said, Janssen would still probably continue to argue that its label is adequate, and that gynecomastia isn't a serious adverse event.

The Risperdal warning that should have been given would have alerted doctors to check prolactin levels in a child before they began to take the drug and then at intervals of two, six and eight weeks. If levels are elevated after two months, the child should be taken off the drug.

Woodcock refused to entertain what I considered to be a responsible warning.

Also, since the company and FDA knew that most kids on Risperdal would put on excessive weight, parents and doctors should have been warned that weight gain masks gynecomastia. Parents instead were led to believe that their kid was simply getting fat when in reality the fat was breast tissue. Doctors and patients should have been warned that a specialized breast and chest exam was needed to distinguish between the two.

Abnormal prolactin is not a good thing for a child! Usually an ultra- sound and/or biopsy could have determined whether the child had gynecomastia. None of those points made it into a warning.

We know from the label and its current warnings that at least 50 percent of children on the drug would have had abnormal prolactin levels on early tests in the first three months. We also know that those with abnormal prolactin levels at weeks eight through 12 were the ones with much greater risk of developing gynecomastia if they continued to use Risperdal, according to the infamous Table 21 the company hid from doctors and the FDA. In fact, their chance of developing the condition jumped from 5.5 percent during year one to 12.5 percent after two years.

There's a word for what drove the corruption we uncovered at every step along the way of this case: greed. The greater question is what we are going to do about it collectively.

Janssen won't change course unless pushed. We scored at least one victory in that direction when a Pennsylvania appeals court overturned Judge New's decision on punitive damages and opened the door for plaintiffs to seek those awards yet again. In a unanimous decision in January 2018, a three-judge panel ruled that plaintiffs may apply the laws of their home states in an attempt to obtain a punitive damage award.

The ruling came in a case involving Wisconsin resident Timothy Stange, who began taking Risperdal at age 12 to treat his Tourette's syndrome. Stange, who developed gynecomastia, would eventually have surgery to remove his breasts. Jurors awarded him $500,000 in damages in October 2015, but he was barred by New's order from seeking additional compensation. Punitive damages, imposed for the purpose of punishing corporate wrongdoers, would go a long way to achieving justice for Stange.

Our victory in Stange's appeal, however sweet, may be short-lived as I've seen no evidence of responsibility on Janssen's part and the company has shown its willingness to fight to avoid responsibility, fighting at the appellate level what it can't win at the trial stage. As a consequence, the cases of thousands of children are being held hostage while the company continues to maneuver a way out of liability for injuries that its product caused.

AFTERWORD: TAKING BACK CONTROL FROM BIG PHARMA

For all his skill at finance and logistics, oil baron John D. Rockefeller had one other distinctive trait – his instinct for ruthlessly crushing the competition.

After reaping enormous profits with a small shipping business during the Civil War, Rockefeller invested in Cleveland area refineries that made kerosene from crude oil that came from nearby Pennsylvania oil wells. Kerosene then was rapidly replacing whale oil, which was more expensive and subject to frequent shortages, as the primary fuel for oil lamps in millions of homes and business. Rockefeller correctly reasoned there were enormous profits to be made supplying this market.

Once the refinery system was in place along with a distribution network, he rapidly scaled the business to major cities across the nation.

Then he set about crushing competing refineries. Rockefeller undercut competitors on price by arranging secret discounts with railroads. He bought up parts and supplies that prevented other refiners from operating, bribed Pennsylvania legislators and later in the business cycle, took control of the pipeline system so that he could cut off supplies to competitors.

Rockefeller justified these predations by saying a monopoly business delivered products with greater efficiency and cost effectiveness than a marketplace composed of competing businesses that waste resources by duplicating efforts. But the public, appalled at Rockefeller's strong-arm tactics and price manipulation, didn't see it that way, nor did Congress and the courts.

In 1911, the United States Supreme Court ordered the breakup of Rockefeller's Standard Oil Co., finding that it violated the Sherman Antitrust Act by illegally snuffing out business rivals.

Is it perhaps too much to imagine that a similar fate awaits the pharmaceutical industry?

There are, of course, important differences between the marauding excesses of Standard Oil, the railroads and other trusts of that era. Big pharma companies, for one, have the legal right to run a monopoly business. In 1983, Congress authorized years of patent exclusivity for new medications as an inducement for drug companies to invest in research and development. The idea was that a period of patent protection would fuel the entrepreneurial zeal of drug makers. But in case after case, drug companies have abused that power by gouging customers, foisting dangerous medicines on the public, converting respected health journals into little more than propaganda organs and thoroughly compromising the regulatory agencies whose supposed mission it is to protect public health.

In less than half a decade, our firm was substantially responsible for four of the top eight Big Pharma whistleblower settlements of all time, a sum exceeding $6 billion.

However, as much I would like to celebrate, I can't claim victory. Newer and potentially more lethal pharmaceuticals enter the market each month, and the corporate titans with whom I do battle become ever more powerful and cunning.

Drug company executives continue to manipulate test results, ghostwrite reviews of their own products, influence physicians into doing their bidding, and lobby legislators and the judiciary to roll back initiatives put in place to regulate them. All the while, the victims of their fraud die or are injured in ever greater numbers. Yet these are the same companies to whom we entrust our health.

What's needed is a sweeping reform of the industry and the agencies that regulate it, including:

- Institution of price controls, much like those in the European Union.
- A top to bottom restructuring and repurposing of the

FDA aimed at restoring its independence.

■ Elimination of so called "me too" drugs, compounds with the same physiological effects as cheaper drugs that are already on the market.

■ A flat out ban on drug advertising.

■ Having the government, in concert with teaching hospitals and university labs, conduct clinical trials, not drug manufacturers. As a general rule, Big Pharma should be kept out of university labs.

■ Revoke the corporate charters of drug companies that repeatedly develop and market, under false pretenses, dangerous drugs.

Given the backdrop of industry abuses, no agency of the federal government is more in need of an overhaul than the FDA. Our primary pharmaceutical regulatory agency must not continue to be the Big Pharma alumni club, in which pharmaceutical executives go to work for the FDA—oftentimes making regulatory decisions on matters affecting their industry and sometimes even their own companies—and then go back to higher-paying jobs in the drug industry.

Against this backdrop, lobbyists and lobbying are unnecessary because there is no middleman between the regulators and the influence peddlers. In fact, the conflict of interest is mandatory: by law, industry representatives have to sit on the FDA's so-called "independent" scientific advisory committees, and FDA administrators must, by law, consult and negotiate with the industry on the agency's goals and plans.

Let's be honest about the conflict of interest and do something about it. A significant time limit must be put in place on how soon a former FDA employee or scientist can receive funding or be employed in the industry – say five years. Better still, let's recruit scientists and administrators whose dedication is to our nation's health, not the industry's bottom line.

We must also produce high-quality clinical trials that the FDA can use to evaluate the safety and efficacy of a new drug.

The problem here is that the pharmaceutical companies now

conduct, oversee, and subsidize nearly all clinical testing. As we have seen, they select the trial participants, stop testing that would cast their products in an unfavorable light (and bury the evidence that testing even took place), decide who sees the raw data, choose what findings are submitted to the FDA, and contract with "opinion leaders" to publish favorable reviews in prestigious, high-impact journals.

And if being both the judge and jury weren't enough, the clinical trial markers that the FDA uses to determine a drug's efficacy couldn't be any lower. The drug sponsor must only demonstrate that their product is an improvement, however marginal, over taking a placebo, which, in essence, is doing almost nothing, in most instances.

Beyond certain moral issues—such as whether or not human guinea pigs should be paid to participate in corporate-sponsored drug trials—I have no objection to drug companies or any other corporation testing their products. The more testing the better! To my mind, however, such testing should only be the starting point—that which the FDA should use to determine a new drug's *eligibility* to begin the approval process. Otherwise, the temptation for Big Pharma to manipulate the evidence is too great. The common-sense next step would be for the FDA to conduct its own third-party, independent testing.

The emphasis here would be on health as an inalienable right in our nation, not big businesses where a handful of corporations play puppet master. Rather than working for the pharmaceutical industry—which, in essence, is what the FDA is now doing—it would be working for the American people.

The most suitable candidates to partner with the government would be teaching hospitals and university laboratories and those we can presume to be less inclined to pander to pharmaceutical-industry imperatives. As an added safeguard and as a condition of FDA certification, researchers and their institutions wouldn't be permitted to accept pharmaceutical company subsidies or sponsorships. And just as the volunteers or paid trial participants aren't told what specific drugs or treatments they are being given, the trial conductors wouldn't know which company is producing the drug being tested.

Equally important, the results of the trials would belong to the

U.S. government and not Big Pharma. Physicians and researchers everywhere would be able to see and learn from the data.

By conducting its own clinical trials, the FDA would also have the freedom to design its own protocols. Approval would not be based only on whether taking the drug is better than taking a placebo, but whether the new drug is a significant improvement over previously approved drugs, time-tested treatments, and holistic therapies.

How do the risks and benefits of a new diabetes drug, for example, compare to a change in diet and moderate exercise? How does a new prescription pain reliever compare to taking an over-the-counter aspirin? Does a new cancer treatment extend a patient's life or simply mask the symptoms of the disease? How many years would it take a patient using a new osteoporosis drug to build enough bone density to warrant taking it? You would logically think such basic questions are addressed in clinical trials, but they rarely are. One of the reasons is that the new "miracle" drugs don't measure up to industry claims, and the drug producer would rather the consumers and their physicians not know it. The drug companies also have no financial incentive to comparison test their products with traditional, centuries-old remedies or drugs that are no longer in patent, and hence cannot become the private property of the drug producer. For example, a change in diet for sufferers of psoriasis and other skin-related conditions may be a far more effective treatment than prescription topical ointments. Only you will not know this from drug-company-sponsored clinical trials.

Another advantage over the old system would be the huge cost savings and health benefits as a result of the decreasing number of "me too" drugs put on the market. The pharmaceutical companies would be less inclined to produce these copycat drugs because they would have to prove that their formulations are better than the ones they copied. The effort spent to produce such drugs could then be channeled into truly innovative research. Who knows? Maybe a Renaissance in medical breakthroughs would result.

The pharmaceutical industry (as well as the politicians in its pocket) will naturally argue that the federal government ought to stay out of the business of conducting clinical research, that corporations can do the job more efficiently and at a lower cost. Overwhelming evidence suggests otherwise. A recent survey has shown that university hospitals can perform drug trials that are more reliable and for an estimated one-tenth to one-twentieth of the cost of industry trials.[59] Beyond these advantages, there would be the added benefit of increased cash flow to academic institutions and medical professionals who presumably will no longer be under pressure to massage test results in ways that benefit drug makers but deceive the public.

How much would it cost the American taxpayer to empower the FDA to conduct clinical trials? One hospital researcher with extensive clinical trial experience has estimated that levying a 2 percent tax on prescription medications would quickly create a fund large enough to cover the entire process.[60] Several European governments accomplish the same thing by taxing the pharmaceutical industry itself.[61] But whatever system is put into place to finance testing, the net results would cost considerably less than what consumers already pay in the form of inflated drug prices. This much we know for certain, thanks in no small part to price-fixing investigations.

As we have seen, a pill costing the manufacturer a mere $0.11 to produce is routinely sold for $25. And the alleged $800 million or more that the industry routinely claims to put into research and development to develop a new drug is less than $100 million.[62]

Clinical trials aside, there are plenty of other ways the system needs to be revamped. One much needed reform would be giving FDA regulators complete access to all corporate-sponsored drug tests and data associated with them.

Further, FDA researchers should have access to pharmaceutical archives to mine the results of past trials. Such oversight of corporate records is routine for the IRS. Why shouldn't other government regulators, such as the FDA, have access to Big Pharma's records? GlaxoSmithKline has promised this, and it may very well live up to its promise, but all the drug companies need to follow suit.

Transparency must be the rule, not the exception. Thankfully, the passage of the Sunshine Act, which is part of the Affordable Care Act and was put into effect in 2013, is a major step in the right direction. This act requires drug manufacturers and producers of medical devices and supplies to report payments, ownership, investment interests, and other transfers of value they make to physicians and teaching hospitals. You and I need only go to the CMS.gov website to see the potential conflicts of interest a physician might have. I would go the next logical step and mandate that drug companies also declare all payments, subsidies, and advertising that they give medical societies, groups, and associations, as occurred in Kentucky when NAMI was helping Eli Lilly keep Zyprexa on the preferred-drug list. If corporate sponsorship makes it possible for a society or association to host continuing education junkets at tropical resorts or expensive restaurants, such payments must be declared and the event ought to be called what it is: a sales conference.

Along these same lines, medical journals and other forms of medical knowledge dissemination must admit the disservice they are doing to the public by publishing obviously biased writers and accepting ghostwritten reviews and reports. As Dr. John Abramson from Harvard Medical School has pointed out, this shouldn't be a game of cat and mouse in which corporate sponsors do their best to hide the ways that their scientific results have been spun.[63] Medical journals in particular must adhere to far higher scientific standards because millions of lives hang in the balance. Doing otherwise would ultimately result in public disregard for physicians in general. Former *New England Journal of Medicine* editor Dr. Jerome Kassirer, an advocate of higher ethical standards, stated this best: "At issue is whether the public can trust us not only to be at their side but on their side."[64]

Another necessary reform would prohibit direct-to-consumer advertising of prescription drugs on television, radio, print media and on the Internet.

Despite pronouncements to the contrary, it's simply delusional to believe that the purpose of these ads is to enliven discussion between a patient and his or her physician, as the ads purport to do. Their purpose is to sell drugs, which they do by lulling viewers into believing the medications they are being sold are safe and effective; otherwise, the companies wouldn't be advertising it. The bottom line is this: if the drugs were entirely safe, they wouldn't require a prescription, and just because they have been approved by the FDA doesn't mean they're effective or safe. A consumer simply can't evaluate the efficacy of a particular drug in a thirty-second TV spot, which is why the practice is outlawed in all advanced countries except the United States and New Zealand. As the *New York Times* has aptly put it, "Consumer advertising, delivered to the masses as a shotgun blast, rather than as specific information to concerned patients or caregivers, results in more prescriptions and less appropriate prescribing."[65]

That's why the drug companies do it and why it must be stopped.

New laws must also be put in place to regulate the widespread practice of prescribing drugs off-label. The practice—with few exceptions—should be banned altogether. After all, if a drug hasn't been proven safe for a particular use, then it ought not be prescribed for that use. In certain life-or-death instances, however, or if a physician is convinced beyond any doubt that it is the right drug to prescribe to their patient at that time, then the physician ought to be permitted to prescribe it. However, he or she should rightfully first obtain a legal consent form signed by their patient as evidence that the patient is aware they are being prescribed a drug that has not been approved by the FDA for that purpose and is also aware of the potential side effects (which could be listed on the consent form in easy-to-understand language). The emphasis here should be on physician responsibility and, perhaps too, liability. Remember Gabriel Myers, who underwent examinations that lasted for two or three minutes before he was prescribed what turned out to be a deadly drug cocktail? If a physician believes he or she may have to explain to a jury why they made the decision, there would be fewer off-label prescriptions written.

Further, as we saw in the Austin Pledger case, had there been adequate labeling on drug packaging, there would likely not have been an off-label prescription written. Drug labels and packaging must clearly present all possible side effects organized according to their degree of severity—and I don't mean in print so small that a consumer must squint to read the individual words or written with such convoluted terminology and phrasing that even the doctors themselves are confused by what is being communicated. Manufacturers must be legally obligated to list all the potential side effects, which side effects are the most serious, and the percentages of individuals taking the drug who have suffered such side effects. Further, this information must be presented to both patient and physician—if not in a clearly and easily understood booklet accompanying each prescription, then in an electronic form available on the Internet.

Drug pricing is another long-overdue reform. Why is it that drugs are 50 percent less expensive in Europe? Why shouldn't Medicare and Medicaid comparison shop for the best drug prices? The answer to all of these questions is the same: drug companies selling their products in the United States can charge whatever price they want and know that our insurers and health care system will pay for it.

Thanks to drug industry-sponsored media hype, we are told that our health care providers must make all products available to everyone regardless of the price. Otherwise, we will have "death panels." Such a fallacy belies the overwhelming evidence from abroad. Health care systems in Europe and Canada, which are more selective about the effectiveness of the drugs they permit to be marketed and invite competition into the equation, provide better health care and less-expensive drugs. The United States should do the same by demanding that the FDA raise its scientific standards, compel financial regulators to put a stop to price-fixing, and motivate legislators to level the playing field by putting a stop to the many special interest rules and regulations that are voted into law every year.

It's time as well for a much more aggressive law-enforcement approach. I do not mean just leveling a fine, for clearly a financial penalty is not enough. The chief executives of these companies will continue to commit illegal or unethical acts and encourage their subordinates to do the same as the "cost of doing business" until they themselves are held criminally accountable.

A surefire way to move this reform forward is to remove immunity from prosecution as a bargaining chip in cases involving criminal activities such as medical fraud, lying to federal officials, bribery, and failure to disclose life-threatening adverse effects. Those engaged in wrongdoing need to be held personally liable and face federal prison for their crimes. Because of decisions these executives make—oftentimes driven by the tens of millions of dollars in bonus compensation they receive—people die. That's manslaughter. Don't issue these bad actors a "get out of jail free" card just because they can afford to buy one.

I would go even further in this regard: if a company and its executives are serial offenders, not only should the chief officers go to jail, but the company should also forfeit future profits or patent rights to some or all of the drugs it is producing. In particularly egregious instances, I would go to the extreme of issuing a corporate death penalty. By this, I mean the charters giving corporations license to operate should be revoked. This is not only legally feasible, but it's morally justified when many hundreds and potentially millions of people are harmed because scientific data has been manipulated or marketers are knowingly bringing an inferior and dangerous product to market. Although I will be the first to admit that charter revocation hasn't yet been applied to multinational corporate lawbreakers the way it has commonly been used to hold small companies liable for injurious behavior, I don't see any reason not to try. Loyola Law School professor Robert Benson attempted to do this to Union Oil of California (Unocal) in the aftermath of a massive oil spill and numerous wanton acts of pollution in the 1960s. If Unocal's charter had been revoked, perhaps BP would have taken greater precautions and there wouldn't have been the 2010 Deepwater Horizon oil spill in the Gulf of Mexico.

"People mistakenly assume that we have to try to control these giant corporate repeat offenders…[only with fines] but the law has always allowed the attorney general to go to court to simply dissolve a corporation for wrongdoing and sell its assets to others who will operate in the public interest," Professor Benson wrote.[lxxi]

Pharmaceutical chieftains will claim that their companies are too large and too important to be dissolved. The health of the nation depends on them. But consider, if you will, how twisted this logic is. It's akin to saying we must tolerate criminal behavior as the price for our own (ill) health, which of course is entirely nonsensical. The truth of the matter is that we don't have to tolerate injustice. Nor do we need worry that our continued health depends upon these corporations. Any lifesaving or life-enhancing medications these companies produce can, by court order, be turned over to others for generic drug production.

The greater challenge is mustering the political will necessary to bring about such changes. Simply accomplishing one of these, such as making all drug studies and the data associated with them available to the FDA or putting criminal offenders behind bars, would be enough to bring significant improvements. But the problem here is the close relationship between the drug manufacturers and legislators.

Data compiled by the Center for Responsive Politics and commissioned by the Union of Concerned Scientists shows that between 1998 and 2013, pharmaceutical and health-product manufacturers spent nearly $3 billion lobbying lawmakers, making them the single largest contributor to legislative efforts, among all industries.[66] Of the hundreds of registered pharmaceutical lobbyists, dozens are former members of Congress. One former member, Republican Billy Tauzin, was paid $11 million in salary, making him the highest paid lobbyist on the Hill.[lxxiii] And while we're talking big numbers: between 2009 and 2011, prescription drug, biotechnology, and medical device companies spent more than $700 million specifically lobbying Congress and the White House.[67] That's the equivalent of spending over $1 million dollars for each congressman and senator on Capitol Hill!

Such huge sums cause one to ask, what are the pharmaceutical chieftains getting in return for their investments? Among the most obvious benefits are predatory pricing practices, which include bans on the importation of pharmaceuticals (at a fraction of American prices) and a provision that prevents Medicare and Medicaid from finding the best prices for the billions they spend on drugs. Then, of course, there are the Big Pharma alumni appointments to government regulatory advisory boards. I've previously mentioned the former executives at both Lilly and J&J on such boards, but the sad truth is that there are so many others that, as one insider remarked, it would be difficult to find anyone with authority who wasn't connected in some way to the corporations they seek to regulate.

Equally alarming are the industry-friendly legislative proposals that routinely go before the House and Senate. In recent years, I have seen initiatives that would erode the FDA's standard of substantial evidence when reviewing drugs and medical devices, legislation that would relax conflict-of-interest standards for federal advisory committee members at the FDA, and the restricting of whistleblower statutes. Then, there is legislation that would restrict the ability of state attorneys general to partner with plaintiffs' attorneys. Imagine the consequences if such legislation is passed. It was precisely because of the partnerships I made with state attorneys general that we successfully took on Big Tobacco and the pharmaceutical giants.

Make no mistake: the business of health care is big business, not health care. This is why pharmaceutical companies are not only funding the political campaigns of our senators and congressmen, but they're also working on state and local levels to fund the campaigns of judges who will likely be more receptive to their company's interests. Spearheading the so-called judicial "reform" movement is the secretive Civil Justice Reform Group (CJRG), which is comprised of the general counsels of some of the largest and most profitable corporations in the world. Among the group representatives are senior executives from Aetna, AT&T, BP, Bristol-Myers Squibb, Chevron, Chrysler, Citibank, DuPont, Exxon, Ford, General Electric, General Motors, GlaxoSmithKline, Koch Cos., Merck & Co., Pfizer, Procter & Gamble, State Farm, Texaco, W. R. Grace, and, you guessed it, J&J. Remember Merck's Vioxx, W.R. Grace's asbestos products, Ford's exploding Pinto, and BP's oil spill in the Gulf of Mexico? Corporate executives knew of the dangers yet continued to sell the products or services to unsuspecting consumers.[68]

Now we can add Janssen's Risperdal to the list.

Sadly, conditions may have to get considerably worse before they can get better. This appears to be the case in my own hometown of Philadelphia where, thanks to lobbying efforts, corporate profits are taking precedence over the sick and needy. For as long as I can remember, competent Philadelphia judges kept the courthouse doors open to injured individuals and cases moving forward in a timely way. Now, it appears judges are under tacit orders to make it more difficult for plaintiffs to bring cases, to receive fair compensation for injuries, or to punish wrongdoing corporations by assessing punitive damages. As a commenter for the Pennsylvania Association for Justice has said, "If changes to the courts are good news to a group funded by Big Tobacco, insurance companies, and pharmaceutical firms...is that good news for anyone else?"[69]

This brings me back to where I started: the disputed Bush versus Gore election and what more I could and should have done to demand that justice was served. Democracy is not a spectator sport. Not until we exercise our rights and move others to awareness and to action can we protect the Gabriel Meyers of the world. He and countless others injured by the pharmaceutical industry aren't the only victims of the fraud. All of us are. Don't become one of the many who will look back on what has happened and ask, "What were we thinking? How could this possibly have all come about?" Rather, look back and be proud of what you did to be a voice of conscience and justice in a time when we need those two timeless verities more than ever.

ACKNOWLEDGMENTS

Clarence Darrow once said, "As long as the world shall last, there will be wrongs, and if no man rebelled, those wrongs would last forever."

I thank the many men and women who inherently follow this principle and have set higher standards for seeking justice with integrity. Early on in my life, Dr. Thomas G. Lawrence, my science teacher from Erasmus Hall High School in Brooklyn, and Drs. Marvin Wolfgang and John Honnold, professors at the University of Pennsylvania, taught me the value of seeking truth with integrity through science and law.

As a young lawyer, Reverend Paul Washington's tenacity to protect all people and do what is right with integrity despite being challenged greatly encouraged me. Judges Edmund Spaeth, Raymond Pace Alexander, and Alexander Barbieri set the standard that enabled me to understand how the judiciary and legal system can protect our citizens with justice in the most difficult situations.

I owe gratitude to Judges Sandra Mazer Moss and William Manfredi for being loyal and consistent friends and sounding boards over many years of my legal practice, keeping me on the straight and narrow. I thank former Governor Edward Rendell for demonstrating how good political leadership can result in justice, and for advancing hope and benefit for the majority of citizens.

Fellow attorneys who worked with me on these various cases, Mike Mustokoff, Mark Lipowicz, Mark Aronchick, Teresa Cavenagh, Michael Freedland, and Gary Farmer, added so much to my analysis of what could be done and the success of what we accomplished. Our Risperdal litigation partner Tom Kline continues to seek justice for our individual Risperdal gynecomastia clients. Steven Brill's 15-part "docuserial" 'America's Most Admired Lawbreaker', published by the Huffington Post's Highline division, delves deeply into the history of Johnson and Johnson's marketing of Risperdal. I thank him for his dedication to providing the journalistic exposé and appreciate his including me in the narrative.

A special note of thanks to Valerie Jones for her integral role in shaping this manuscript including delving into, researching and finding documents and materials that would elude most investigative reporters. Her wise counsel and invaluable input are on every page. Also, a shout out to Christopher Naughton, former prosecutor, trial attorney and host of the Emmy award-winning television program *The American Law Journal*, for providing a forum in which consumer protection, constitutional rights and so many of the issues dear to my heart can be openly discussed and debated.

Dr. David Kessler, past commissioner of the FDA, joined me early on in my career in the tobacco fight and has been forthright in standing up for justice in the pharmaceutical litigation.

Bobbie Mitnik, my wife's mother, was also a tenacious champion of doing what's right. Her unwillingness to accept injustice on any level was what led me to call the state of Florida to task over the troubled butterfly ballot.

Equally courageous have been my many clients—to name a few who inspire me even today, I thank Benita Pledger, Victoria Starr, and James Wetta for their unwavering commitment to justice and integrity for themselves, their families, and all families, despite the hardships they met with in the process.

Finally, I thank the unwavering support and love of my family, who understands my passion for justice and carries the torch with me: my wife, Sandy and my daughters, Jamie, Mimi, Danielle, and Lauren. My hope is that their children, my grandchildren—Dane, Beau, Ally, Eve, and Hudson—will continue the quest.

STEPHEN A. SHELLER

ABOUT THE AUTHORS

Stephen A. Sheller is a prominent, Philadelphia-based plaintiffs' lawyer and political activist whose pioneering litigation against the tobacco industry and pharmaceutical companies resulted in multibillion-dollar verdicts and brought about widespread reforms.

As a young lawyer in Philadelphia in the 1970s, Sheller took on government and corporate actors, from defending Black Panthers rounded up in an illegal police raid to protecting the rights of African American women in one of the nation's first equal pay for equal work cases. Later, in the 2000 presidential election, he was in the vanguard of lawyers challenging voting procedures in the Bush v. Gore litigation on behalf of former Vice President Al Gore in Broward County in Florida, triggering a statewide recount.

But it was in his legal battles with the drug industry that Sheller met his most severe test and arguably achieved his greatest results.

In January of 2009, drug maker Eli Lilly pleaded guilty to illegally marketing the anti-psychotic medication Zyprexa and settled lawsuits against it for $1.42 billion, the largest amount ever paid by any one defendant and, at the time, the largest single drug settlement in US history. That remarkable result was followed by settlements with Pfizer for $2.3 billion and Astra Zeneca, in litigation over its drug, Seroquel, for $520 billion.

A few years later, in 2013, then-U.S. Attorney General Eric Holder announced that Johnson & Johnson had settled with the government for $2.2 billion over claims that it had illegally marketed Risperdal, a second generation anti-psychotic implicated in the growth of female breast tissue in young boys who had been prescribed the drug. Sheller and his firm, Sheller, P.C., had initiated the whistleblower lawsuit based on damning testimony from company insiders and internal documents showing J&J suppressed information about the drug's risk even as it illegally marketed the drug for use in children.

In addition to his legal work, Sheller is active in philanthropic circles. He and his wife, Sandra, established the Sheller Family Foundation whose initiatives have included a family health services center in Philadelphia for underserved populations, the Stephen and Sandra Sheller Center for Social Justice at Temple University's Beasley School of Law and many other projects. In 2017, Sheller received, from Drexel University, the Degree of Doctor of Humane Letters honoris causa for his service and work.

Sidney D. Kirkpatrick is an award-winning documentary filmmaker and a bestselling author. His documentaries include *My Father the President*. His books include *A Cast of Killers*; *Turning the Tide: One Man Against the Medellin Cartel* (with Peter Abrahams); and *The Revenge of Thomas Eakins*, among other works.

Chris Mondics is a legal affairs journalist and former Washington correspondent for The Philadelphia Inquirer whose work on both domestic and international subjects has appeared in the Los Angeles Times, Chicago Tribune, the Washington Post and many other publications.

Index

2000 presidential election, 9–13, 81. *see also* Bush v. Gore

AACAP. *see* American Academy of Child and Adolescent Psychiatry (AACAP)
Abilify, 7, 33, 60
Abramson, John, 121
Adderall XR, 1
ADHD. *see* attention deficit hyperactivity disorder (ADHD)
advertising
  ban on, 117, 121–22
  to children, 5, 7, 47, 68, 107
  direct-to-consumer, 24
  "doctor shopping" and, 25
  in drug company budget, 24
  misleading, 24–26
  "off label" prescribing and, 54
  regulation of, 25–26
  research as, 31–32
  side effects in, 25
Affordable Care Act, 120
Alexis, Aaron, 4
Alliance for Human Research Protection, 76
American Academy of Child and Adolescent Psychiatry (AACAP), 73, 76, 110
American Journal of Medicine, 35
American Journal of Psychiatry, 35, 62
American Psychiatric Association, 110
Amylin Pharmaceuticals, 14
Andreasen, Nancy, 35
Andrews, Robert, 29
Angell, Marcia, 31–32
Anti-Kickback Statute, 48
antipsychotics, 33–36, 62–64, 68–72, 76, 84, 95
arbitration, 96–97
Arthur Andersen (accounting firm), 107
AstraZeneca, 5, 7, 33, 46–50, 51, 62, 67, 72, 106
attention deficit hyperactivity disorder (ADHD), 1–2, 64, 65, 71, 73. *see also* Risperdal
atypical antipsychotics, 33–36, 46, 50, 62–63, 68–70, 76, 82, 95
autism, 59, 64, 71
Avandia, 91
Azar, Alex, 14

Bad Ad outreach program, 25–26
Ballard Spahr (law firm), 96
Barry, Kurtis J., 55
Bayer Corp, 23
Becker, Charles, 6
Benjamin, Eric, 72

Benson, Robert, 124
Bextra, 49
Biederman, Joseph, 64–66, 74, 76, 110
Biotechnology Innovation Organization, 92
bipolar disorder, 47–48, 64–66, 101
Boies, David, 12
Buchanan, Pat, 9–10, 11
Bush, George H. W., 13–14
Bush, George W., 11, 14, 29, 81, 83, 105
Bush, Jeb, 11
Bush v. Gore, 12, 49

Caers, Ivo, 111–12
Center for Drug Evaluation and Research, 35, 76, 90
Center for Responsive Politics, 125
CEO. *see* chief executive officer (CEO)
CFPB. *see* Consumer Financial Protection Bureau (CFPB)
chief executive officer (CEO) compensation, 109
children. *see also* Risperdal
   advertising to, 5, 7, 47, 68, 107
   diagnosis of mental disorders among, 4, 64, 83–84
   foster, 1–3, 5, 7–8, 39
   "off-label" prescribing and, 2
   production of drugs more easily administered to, 73–74
cigarettes, 43–44
Citizens United, 13
Civil Justice Reform Group (CJRG), 126
CJRG. *see* Civil Justice Reform Group (CJRG)
class actions, 96–97
clinical trials, 36, 90, 93, 117–20. *see also* research
Columbine High School massacre, 4
Consumer Financial Protection Bureau (CFPB), 96–97
Cordray, Richard, 97
Coumadin, 27
credit cards, 96–97
Cymbalta, 84

Daneman, Denis, 7
Daniels, Mitch, 14
Daubert v. Merrell Dow, 36
Davis, Legrome, 112
"death panels," 123
Defense Department, 49
Depakote, 4
depression, 16–18, 28, 34, 47, 84
DES, 34
diabetes, 4, 32, 35–36, 37, 41, 48, 66, 119
dietary supplements, 85–88
doctors. *see* physicians

"doctor shopping," 25
Doetterl, Judy, 55
drug prices
  control of, 116
  generics and, 27
  illicit payments and, 23
  reform of, 122–23
  reformulation and, 23–24
  testing and, 120
drug reformulation, 23–24
drug representatives. *see* sales representatives

Ebbers, Bernie, 106
Egilman, David, 40
Eli Lilly, 5, 7, 13–15, 29, 35–36, 38–42, 44–45, 51, 54, 84, 121. See also Prozac
EMS. *see* eosinophilia-myalgia syndrome (EMS)
Energy and Commerce Committee, 91–92
Enron, 14, 105–6
eosinophilia-myalgia syndrome (EMS), 87
Excerpta Medica, 62, 67–68, 72–73, 78
Exelon, 109–10

False Claims Act, 44–46, 48, 49, 84
Farmer, Gary, 10, 13, 14, 18, 29, 31, 37, 49
Fastow, Andy, 106
Federal False Claims Act, 44–46, 48, 49, 84
Findling, Robert, 7
Fiorello, Steve, 81–83
Flonase, 26
Food, Drug and Cosmetic Act, 92
Food and Drug Administration (FDA)
  advertising and, 25–26
  Big Pharma influence on, 89–91
  and Bush, George H.W., 13
  Center for Drug Evaluation and Research, 35, 76, 90
  clinical trials and, 118–20
  dietary supplements and, 87–88
  Eschenbach and, 14
  Office of New Drugs, 90
  and "off label" prescribing, 2
  and Prescription Drug User Fee Act, 92
  reform of, 63, 116–17
  refusal to review information, 111–12
  Risperdal and, 63–64, 75–77
formaldehyde, 108
Foster, John, 23
foster children, 1–3, 5, 7–8, 39
Freedland, Michael, 31
frontal lobe, 35

Frye v. United States, 36
Fullmer, Charlene K., 51

generics
   court-ordered production of, 124
   drug prices and, 27
   for Prozac, 21–22
   for Risperdal, 73, 110, 111
Geodon, 4, 5, 7, 33, 48, 49–50, 52, 60
Gibson, Virginia A., 45
Gilead Sciences, 14
GlaxoSmithKline, 24, 26, 91, 120
Global Prolactin Task Force, 69–70
Gore, Al, 9–10, 11, 12
Gorsky, Alex, 79, 109–10
Graham, David, 89–90
Greenwood, James, 91–92
gynecomastia, 4, 6, 57–61, 67–73, 100, 102–4, 111–14

Hager, Destiny, 4–5, 7–8, 64, 70
Haldol, 33, 63
Hamburg, Margaret, 111
Harris, Katherine, 10, 11
Health and Human Services (HHS), 14, 45
Health Care Fraud Prevention and Enforcement Action Team (HEAT), 45
HEAT. *see* Health Care Fraud Prevention and Enforcement Action Team (HEAT)
HHS. *see* Health and Human Services (HHS)
Holder, Eric, 79. *see also* Justice Department
Homeland Security Act, 29
House Energy and Commerce Committee, 91–92
House Subcommittee on Oversight and Investigations, 91–92

illicit payments, 23–24. *see also* kickbacks
inducements, 26, 36, 55. *see also* kickbacks
Invega, 5, 7, 33, 53, 68, 79, 110, 111

Janssen, 6–7, 53, 55–56. *see also* Johnson & Johnson; Risperdal
Johnson, Robert Wood, 57
Johnson & Johnson, 5, 7, 52–56, 57–58. *see also* Janssen; Risperdal
Jones, Allen, 81–85
Jones, Tone, 55–56
Journal of American Psychiatry, 6
Journal of Clinical Psychiatry, 6–7
Journal of the American Academy of Child and Adolescent Psychiatry, 73
Journal of the American Medical Association, 35, 93
journals, 5, 27, 35, 36, 62, 74, 116, 118, 121
"Judicial Hellholes," 95–96
Justice Department, 45, 50–51, 105–8. *see also* Holder, Eric

Kalmeijer, Ronald, 71–72
Kaplinsky, Alan, 96
Kassirer, Jerome, 121
Kefauver-Harris amendments, 92
Kessler, David, 76–77, 101–2
kickbacks, 5, 23, 48, 50. *see also* inducements
Krathen, Dave, 10
Kweder, Sandra, 90

labels, drug, 32, 69, 75, 90, 122
Lambert, Lise, 16, 17, 27
Laughren, Thomas, 76
Lay, Ken, 14, 105
Levaquin, 108
Lexapro, 2
Lincoln Law, 44–46, 48, 84
Lipitor, 26
L-tryptophan, 85–88
Lutwak, Leo, 5
Lyrica, 49

Magid, Laurie, 45
Mahmoud, Ramy, 72
marketing. *see* advertising
mass tort, 101–2
Medicaid, 23, 41–42, 44, 47, 49, 123, 125
medical journals, 5, 27, 35, 36, 62, 74, 116, 118, 121
Medicare, 44, 49, 123, 125
Meehan, Pat, 45
Meibach, Richard, 62
Merck & Co., 26, 50, 89
"me too" drugs, 116–17, 119
military, 14, 49
Mink, Patsy, 87–88
Mitnik, Bobbie, 9–10
monopoly, 115–16
Moss, Sandra, 101
Mulvaney, Mick, 97
Myers, Candace, 1–2
Myers, Gabriel, 1–4, 7, 40–41, 64, 122

NAMI. *see* National Alliance for the Mentally Ill (NAMI)
National Alliance for the Mentally Ill (NAMI), 42, 50, 121
NEJM. *see* New England Journal of Medicine (NEJM)
Neurontin, 50
New, Arnold, 6, 101–3, 102–3, 113
New England Journal of Medicine (NEJM), 31, 121

New Freedom Commission on Mental Health, 83
Newman, Rocky, 2
Novartis, 109

Obama, Barack, 96. *see also* Affordable Care Act
Ochsner Health Plan, 23
ODD. *see* oppositional defiant disorder (ODD)
Office of New Drugs, 90
"off label" prescribing, 2, 31–32, 33–35, 49–50, 52–53, 62, 78–79, 80, 82–83, 122
oppositional defiant disorder (ODD), 65
Osterholm, Michael, 87
Oxycodone, 1–2

Pandina, Gahan, 69–70
Parke-Davis, 23
patent exclusivity, 116
payments, illicit, 23–24. *see also* kickbacks
PDUFA. *see* Prescription Drug User Fee Act (PDUFA)
Pfizer, 5, 7, 23, 26, 49–50
pharmacists
   in Prozac Weekly scam, 22
   as sales representatives, 31
Philadelphia, 95–96
Physician Payment Sunshine Act, 27, 120
physicians
   bribery of, with inducements, 26
   "doctor shopping" for, 25
   on drug company payroll, 27
   kickbacks and inducements to, 5, 23, 48, 50, 55
   "off label" prescribing by, 2, 31–32, 33–35, 49–50, 52–53, 62, 78–79, 80, 82–83, 122
   shill, 36
Pledger, Austin, 59–61, 101–2, 122
Pledger, Benita, 59
Pledger, Philip, 59
polypharmacy, 33, 40–41
Pradaxa, 27
Prescription Drug User Fee Act (PDUFA), 92
presidential election, 2000, 9–13, 81. *see also* Bush v. Gore
prices, drug. *see* drug prices
prolactin, 58, 67–73, 113. *see also* gynecomastia
proprietary information, 7, 98–99
Prozac, 2, 18–19, 33, 60
Prozac Weekly, 16–23, 25, 27–29, 49

Quayle, Dan, 13
Quicksolv, 73–74
qui tam, 44–45, 54, 55

Reagan, Ronald, 14
reform, 63, 116–24
reformulation, 23–24
Rendell, Ed, 10
representatives. *see* sales representatives
research. *see also* clinical trials
    drug prices and, 120
    falsification of, 93
    "me too" drugs and, 119
    "off-label" prescribing and, 31–32
    patent exclusivity and, 116
Riley, Rebecca, 4, 7, 64
Risperdal, 4, 5, 6–7, 33, 48
    approval of, 62–64
    autism and, 71
    bipolar disorder and, 64–65
    deaths from, 75
    gynecomastia from, 57–61, 67–73, 100, 102–4, 111–14
    increasing market share of, to children, 73–74
    legal action over, 52–56, 76–77, 78–79, 97–103, 106–7, 110–14
    protective order with, 97
    sales numbers, 101
Rockefeller, John D., 115–16
Rosado, Hector, 5439
Rudolph, Robert, 39–40
Rumsfeld, Donald, 14

sales representatives
    patient medical records access by, 29–30
    pharmacists as, 31
    in Prozac Weekly scam, 21–22
Seroquel, 4, 5, 7, 33, 46, 47–50, 51, 52, 88, 95
Sherman Antitrust Act, 115–16
Shon, Steven, 83
Showa Denko, 87
side effect(s)
    in advertising, 25
    autism as, 71
    diabetes as, 4, 35–36, 37, 41, 48
    gynecomastia as, 4, 6, 57–61, 67–73, 100, 102–4, 111–14
    "off label" prescribing and, 31–32
    permanent, 35
    polypharmacy and, 33
    violence as, 4
    weight gain as, 4, 34, 41, 48, 53, 60–61, 72, 103–4
Silverstein, Ken, 42
Skilling, Jeffrey, 106
smoking, 43–44

soldiers, 14, 49
Standard Oil, 115–16
Stange, Timothy, 113–14
Starr, Victoria, 53–55
suicide, 1–4, 17, 35, 39–40, 59, 62
sulfanilamide, 92
Sunshine Act, 27, 120
supplements, 85–88
Symbyax, 2

Taurel, Sidney, 14, 29
Tauzin, Billy, 91, 125
Texas Medication Algorithm Project (TMAP), 82–84
thalidomide, 92
third-world countries, sales of obsolete/banned drugs to, 13–14
Thorazine, 33
TMAP. see Texas Medication Algorithm Project (TMAP)
tobacco, 43–44
Trautwein, Joseph, 45
Trump, Donald, 97
Tumas, John, 49

Union of Concerned Scientists, 14, 125
Unocal, 124

vaccines, 27, 29
veterans, 14, 49
violence. see also suicide
  with Prozac, 18–19
  as side effect, 4
Vioxx, 89–90, 126
von Eschenbach, Andrew, 14
Vyvanse, 2

Warfarin, 27
Warner-Lambert Co., 23
Washington Navy Yard shooting, 4
WebMD, 84
weight gain, 4, 34, 41, 48, 53, 60–61, 72, 103–4
Weldon, William, 77, 78–79, 109–10
Wellbutrin XL, 24
Wetta, James, 37–40, 44–45, 46, 48, 50–51
whistleblowers, 23, 38–42, 44–45, 49–50, 53–55
Wilson, Dorothy, 85–87, 88
Woodcock, Janet, 90–91, 111–12
WorldCom, 106
Wray, Christopher, 105–6

Xanax, 1–2
Xarelto, 27

Yount, Andrew, 102

Zoloft, 21
Zyban, 24
Zyprexa, 2, 5, 7, 31–37, 38–40, 48, 51, 121
Zyvox, 49, 52

Notes

[1] "Gabriel Myers DCF Report," 2009, http://www.dcf.state.fl.us/initiatives/GMWorkgroup/docs/GMPresentation.pdf.
[2] Ibid.
[3] Ibid.
[4] "The Real Lesson of Columbine: Psychiatric Drugs Induce Violence," Citizens Commission on Human Rights of Colorado, April 20, 2011, http://psychiatricfraud.org/ 2011/04/the-real-lesson-of-columbine-psychiatric-drugs-induce-violence/.
[5] Shelley Murphy, "Doctor is Sued in Death of Girl, 4," Boston Globe, April 4, 2008.
[6] Evelyn Pringle, "FDA Throws Lifeline to Antipsychotic Pushers," *Counterpunch*, June 12, 2009.
[7] Alice Mundy, *Dispensing with the Truth* (New York: St. Martin's Press, 2001), 52.
[8] R. L. Findling, et al., "Prolactin Levels During Long-Term Risperidone Treatment in Children and Adolescents," *Journal of Clinical Psychiatry*, v. 64(11) November, 2003, pp.1362-9, http://www.ncbi.nlm.nih.gov/pubmed/14658952.
[9] Jesse Mclean and David Bruser, "SickKids doc's impugned study reanalyzed," The Star, March 13, 2016, https://www.thestar.com/news/canada/2016/03/13/sickkids-docs-impugned-study-reanalyzed.html.
[10] 2006–2013, Vitals.com & MDX Medical, Doctor Reviews, http://www.vitals.com/doctors/Dr_Sohail_Punjwani/html.
[11] Martin Merzer, *The Miami Herald Report: Democracy Held Hostage*, (New York: St. Martin's Press, May 2001), 78.
[12] Jeff Gerth, "Bush Tried to Sway a Tax Rule Change But Then Withdrew," *New York Times*, May 19, 1982. http://www.nytimes.com/1982/05/19/business/bush-tried-to-sway-a-tax-rule-change-but-then-withdrew.html?pagewanted=all.
[13] Union of Concerned Scientists: FDA Scientists Survey (2006), http://www.ucsusa.org/our-work/center-science-and-democracy/promoting-scientific-integrity/summary-of-the-fda-scientist.html#.ViKuuRCrRYd.
[14] Tom Watkins, "Papers Indicate Firm Knew Possible Prozac Suicide Risk," *CNN*, January 3, 2005,
http://www.cnn.com/2005/HEALTH/01/03/prozac.documents/index.html.
[15] Richard Zitrin and Carol M. Langford, *The Moral Compass of the American Lawyer: Truth, Justice, Power and Greed* (New York: Ballantine Books, 1999), 193-203.
[16] Adam Liptak, "Free Prozac in the Junk Mail Draws a Lawsuit, *New York Times*, July 6, 2002, http://www.nytimes.com/2002/07/06/us/free-prozac-in-the-junk-mail-draws-a-lawsuit.html.
[17] Mark A. York, "FDA Fails to Cite Big Pharma Opioid Drug Makers for False Marketing and Advertisements," Mass Tort Nexus Media, December 12, 2017, https://www.masstortnexus.com/News/1233/FDA-Fails-to-Cite-Big-Pharma-Opioid-Drug-Makers-for-False-Marketing-and-Advertisements.
[18] Office of the White House Press Secretary, November 25, 2002,
http://georgewbush-whitehouse.archives.gov/news/releases/2002/11/20021125-

6.html.
[19] Katie Thomas, "A Data Trove Now Guides Drug Pitches," *New York Times*, May 17, 2013, https://www.nytimes.com/2013/05/17/business/a-data-trove-now-guides-drug-company-pitches.html?_r=0.
[20] Molly Merrill, "Hospitals 'Struggling' to Protect Patient Data," *Health Care IT News*, November 8, 2010, http://www.healthcareitnews.com/news/hospitals-struggling-protect-patient-data?page=1.
[21] Marcia Angell, *The Truth About the Drug Companies: How They Deceive Us and What To Do About It* (New York: Random House, 2004), p. 305.
[22] Kevin O'Reilly, "Quantifying Adverse Drug Events: Med Mishaps Send Millions Back for Care," *American Medical News*, June 13, 2011, https://amednews.com/article/20110613/profession/306139944/2/.
[23] J. Lazaro et al. and F.H. Gurwitz et al., "Why Learn about Adverse Drug Reactions (ADR)?" Institute of Medicine, National Academy Press, 2000, https://www.fda.gov/Drugs/DevelopmentApprovalProcess/DevelopmentResources/DrugInteractionsLabeling/ucm110632.htm.
[24] The study was published in Archives of Internal Medicine. It was funded by the National Library of Medicine and the Regenstrief Institute, a nonprofit health care research organization affiliated with the Indiana University School of Medicine.
[25] Sovereign Health Sponsored *Psychguides.com*, https://www.psychguides.com/guides/shopping-addiction-treatment-program-options/.
[26] Robert Whitaker, *Anatomy of An Epidemic* (New York: Broadway Books, 2010),113.
[27] Joseph Glenmullen, MD, *The Antidepressant Solution* (New York: Free Press,2006), electronic edition, Chapter 1, Antidepressant Withdrawal and Dependence.
[28] "2012 National Business Ethics Survey," *Ethics Resource Center*, https://www.ethics.org/knowledge-center/2018-gbes/.
See also: Erika Kelton, "The Case Against GE, New Report Shows Real Motive for Attacks on SEC Program," https://www.forbes.com/sites/erikakelton/2012/06/06/whistleblower-case-against-ge-new-report-show-real-motives-for-attacks-on-sec-program/#4c868d2015d5.
A fine introduction to this subject can be found in "The Complete Guide to Snitching," Christopher Matthews, *Wall Street Journal*, December 15, 2011, https://blogs.wsj.com/corruption-currents/2011/12/15/the-complete-guide-to-snitching/.
[29] Miriam Hill, "Whistle-blower's perspective on Lilly case," *Philadelphia Inquirer*, January 19, 2009, https://psychiatricnews.wordpress.com/2009/01/21/the-whistle-blower-who-blew-eli-lilly-out-of-the-water/.

[30] Gardiner Harris, "States Try to Limit Drugs in Medicaid, But Makers Resist," *New York Times*, December 18, 2003, http://www.nytimes.com/2003/12/18/business/states-try-to-limit-drugs-in-medicaid-but-makers-resist.html.

[31] Ken Silverstein, "Prozac.org," *Mother Jones*, November/December 1999, https://www.motherjones.com/politics/1999/11/prozacorg/.

[32] Martha Rosenberg, "Should Your Child Be on Drugs? Yes Says Big Pharma," *Intrepid Report*, October 1, 2012, http://www.intrepidreport.com/archives/7512.

[33] Jim Edwards, "Pfizer Paid for Doc's Helicopter in Off-Label Geodon Push, Suit Claims," *CBS Money Watch*, September 17, 2009, https://www.cbsnews.com/news/pfizer-paid-for-docs-helicopter-in-off-label-geodon-push-suit-claims/.

[34] Milt Freudenheim, Business Technology; Seeking Safer Treatments for Schizophrenia, *New York Times*, January 15, 1992, https://www.nytimes.com/1992/01/15/business/business-technology-seeking-safer-treatments-for-schizophrenia.html.

[35] Risperdal advertisement by Janssen in the *American Journal of Psychiatry*, volume 151 (1994): A111.

[36] FDA warning letters:
http://wayback.archive-it.org/7993/20170111075628/http://www.fda.gov/Drugs/GuidanceComplianceRegulatoryInformation/EnforcementActivitiesbyFDA/WarningLettersandNoticeofViolationLetterstoPharmaceuticalCompanies/ucm482462.htm.

[37] Joseph Biederman biography *Source Watch*, https://www.sourcewatch.org/index.php/Joseph_Biederman.

[38] Press release: "Rates of Bipolar Diagnosis in Youth Rapidly Climbing, Treatment Patterns Similar to Adults," National Institute of Mental Health, September 3, 2007, https://www.nimh.nih.gov/archive/news/2007/rates-of-bipolar-diagnosis-in-youth-rapidly-climbing-treatment-patterns-similar-to-adults.shtml.

[39] Gardiner Harris and Benedict Carey, "Researchers Fail to Reveal Full Drug Pay," New York Times, June 8, 2008, http://www.nytimes.com/2008/06/08/us/08conflict.html.

[40] Biederman deposition:
http://highline.huffingtonpost.com/miracleindustry/americas-most-admired-lawbreaker/assets/documents/8/biederman-depo.pdf.

[41] Rachel Ewing, "In Utero Exposure to Antidepressants May Influence Autism Risk," Drexel NOW News Release,
http://drexel.edu/now/archive/2014/June/Antidepressants-Autism-Risk/.

[42] Kelly Patricia O'Meara, "Honey, They Shrunk My Brain-Study Confirms Antipsychotics Decrease Brain Tissue," CCHR International, The Mental Health Watchdog, https://www.cchrint.org/2013/09/12/honey-they-shrunk-my-brain-study-confirms-antipsychotics-decrease-brain-tissue/.

[43] Research report: "Top FDA Officials Compromised by Conflicts of Interest," Alliance For Human Research Protection, November 9, 2009, http://ahrp.org/top-fda-officials-compromised-by-conflicts-of-interest/.

[44] Ibid.

[45] Michael Bobelian, "J&J's $2.2 Billion Settlement Won't Stop Big Pharma's Addiction To Off-Label Sales," *Forbes*, November 12, 2013, https://www.forbes.com/sites/michaelbobelian/2013/11/12/jjs-2-2-billion-settlement-wont-stop-big-pharmas-addiction-to-off-label-sales/#46993f09515b.

[46] New Freedom Commission Report, https://govinfo.library.unt.edu/mentalhealthcommission/reports/FinalReport/toc.html.

[47] State of Texas ex rel. Jones v. Janssen LP, D-1GV-04-001288, District Court, Travis County, Texas.

[48] CBS Moneywatch, "WebMD's Depression Test Has Only One (Sponsored) Answer: You're "At Risk.", February 22, 2010, http://www.cbsnews.com/news/webmds-depression-test-has-only-one-sponsored-answer-youre-at-risk/.

[49] Martha Rosenberg, OpEdNews.com, "Grassley Investigates Lilly/WebMD link Reported by Washington Post," February 24, 2010, https://www.opednews.com/populum/page.php?f=Grassley-Investigates-Lill-by-Martha-Rosenberg-100224-629.html.

[50] From WebMD's own announcement: Daniel DeNoon, "FDA, WebMD Announce Partnership," December 3, 2008, https://www.webmd.com/a-to-z-guides/news/20081203/fda-webmd-announce-partnership#1.

[51] Bien Jeffrey, Prasad Vinay. Future jobs of FDA's haematology-oncology reviewers, *BMJ* 2016;354:i5055.

[52] Alex Wayne and Drew Armstrong, "Tauzin's $11.6 Million Made Him Highest-Paid Health-Law Lobbyist," *Bloomberg Business*, November 29, 2011, https://www.bloomberg.com/news/articles/2011-11-29/tauzin-s-11-6-million-made-him-highest-paid-health-law-lobbyist.

[53] FDA Consumer Update October 10, 2012: Kefauver-Harris Amendments Revolutionized Drug Development, https://www.fda.gov/ForConsumers/ConsumerUpdates/ucm322856.htm.

[54] Zachary Brennan, "House Passes Bill to Reauthorize FDA Use Fee Programs," *Regulatory Focus*, Regulatory Affairs Professionals Society, July 12, 2017.

[55] David Voreacos and Alex Nussbaum, "J&J Directors Ignored 'Red Flags' on recalls, Probes, Suit Says," *Bloomberg*, December 22, 2010, http://www.bloomberg.com/news/articles/2010-12-21/j-j-directors-accused-by-shareholders-of-ignoring-warnings-before-recalls.

[56] Lorraine Bailey, "Johnson & Johnson CEO 'Grossly' Overpaid As Firm's Reputation Took a Beating, Suit Says," July 19, 2012, *Courthouse News*, http://www.cnssecuritieslaw.com/2012/07/19/458.htm.

[57] Xi Yu, "Three Professors Face Sanctions Following Harvard Medical School

Inquiry," The Harvard Crimson, July 2, 2011.

[58] Ibid.

[59] Bassand J-P, Martyin, Ryden L., et al., "The Need for Resources for Clinical Research," *Lancet* 360 (2002): 1866–9.

[60] Peter Gotzche, *Deadly Medicines and Organized Crime* (Oxford: Radcliffe Medical Press, 2013), electronic edition.

[61] Ibid.

[62] Merrill Goozner, *The 800 Million Pill* (Oakland: University of California Press, 2005) 237, 239.

[63] John Abramson, *Overdosed America: The Broken Promise of American Medicine* (New York: Harper Collins, 2008) 242.

[64] Dr. Jerome Kassirer, *On The Take: How Medicine's Complicity With big Business Can endanger Your Health* (Oxford University Press, 2005) 213.

[65] Kurt Strange, "Consumer Drug Advertising Should Be Banned," *New York Times*, December 16, 2013, https://www.nytimes.com/roomfordebate/2013/12/15/is-the-drug-industry-developing-cures-or-hyping-up-demand/consumer-drug-advertising-should-be-banned.

[66] Top Spenders List "Open Secrets," Center for Responsive Politics, 1998-2016, http://www.opensecrets.org/lobby/indusclient.php?id=H04&year=2016.

[67] Research report "Drug and Medical Device Companies Have Outsized Influence on FDA," Center for Science and Democracy, Union of Concerned Scientists, March 28, 2012, https://www.ucsusa.org/our-work/center-science-and-democracy/promoting-scientific-integrity/drug-companies-influence-FDA.html#.W_MH4ThKiUk.

[68] Wayne Parsons, "Reclaiming Justice: Battling Tort 'Reform,'" *Trial Magazine*, The American Association for Justice, December 2012, http://www.takejusticeback.com/sites/default/files/AAJ%20Trial%20The%20web%20of%20tort%20%E2%80%98reform%E2%80%99.pdf.

[69] News Release "Philadelphia's Removal from 'Judicial Hellhole' List: Who Cares...," Pennsylvania Association for Justice, December 12, 2012, http://communityvoices.post-gazette.com/all-categories/item/35225-philadelphias-removal-from-judicial-hellhole-list-who-cares-what-front.

www.ingramcontent.com/pod-product-compliance
Lightning Source LLC
Chambersburg PA
CBHW020123130526
44591CB00032B/425